D0613884

The Observer's Pocket Series

ROSES

The Observer's Book of

ROSES

MICHAEL GIBSON

WITH 130 COLOUR PHOTOGRAPHS
AND 12 LINE DRAWINGS

BLOOMSBURY BOOKS
LONDON

PENGUIN BOOKS

Published by the Penguin Group
Penguin Books Ltd, 27 Wrights Lane, London W8 5TZ, England
Penguin Books USA Inc., 375 Hudson Street, New York, New York 10014, USA
Penguin Books Australia Ltd, Ringwood, Victoria, Australia
Penguin Books Canada Ltd, 10 Alcorn Avenue, Toronto, Ontario, Canada M4V 3B2
Penguin Books (NZ) Ltd, 182–190 Wairau Road, Auckland 10, New Zealand

Penguin Books Ltd, Registered Offices: Harmondsworth, Middlesex, England

First published by Frederick Warne & Co Ltd 1980

This edition published by Bloomsbury Books, an imprint of
Godfrey Cave Associates Limited, 42 Bloomsbury Street, London, WC1B 3QJ,
under licence from Penguin Books Limited, 1992

3 5 7 9 10 8 6 4 2

Copyright © Michael Gibson 1980

Printed and bound in Great Britain by
BPCC Hazells Ltd
Member of BPCC Ltd

All rights reserved
Without limiting the rights under copyright reserved above,
no part of this publication may be reproduced, stored in or introduced into
a retrieval system, or transmitted, in any form or by any means (electronic,
mechanical, photocopying, recording or otherwise), without the prior
written permission of both the copyright owner and the
above publisher of this book

ISBN 1-8547-1004-4

CONTENTS

ACKNOWLEDGEMENTS

The author and publishers would like to thank Norman Barber for the line drawings and the following for their help in providing the colour photographs for this book: A-Z Botanical Collection for pages 53, 55, 61; R. C. Balfour for pages 52, 88, 89, 90, 101, 110, 137, 147, 164; Pat Brindley for page 63; Cants of Colchester Ltd for pages 68, 80, 128; James Cocker & Sons for pages 66, 95, 117, 150; Dickson Nurseries Ltd for pages 78, 92, 142, 149; C. Gregory & Son Ltd for pages 69, 98, 111, 159, 160, 161; R. Harkness & Co Ltd for pages 67, 118, 124, 127, 133, 140, 154, 158; Harry Smith Collection for pages 51, 58, 99, 100, 120, 166, 170, 173; Robert Pearson for pages 54, 82, 115, 129, 163; The Royal National Rose Society for pages 57, 70, 71, 79, 81, 84, 86, 87, 93, 94, 102, 103, 104, 106, 109, 116, 119, 125, 126, 136, 138, 139, 143, 145, 148, 153; John Sanday (Roses) Ltd for pages 76, 77, 155; Tysterman Photography for pages 72, 132.

The photographs on the following pages are from the author's own collection: 44, 45, 46, 47, 48, 49, 50, 56, 59, 60, 62, 64, 65, 73, 74, 75, 83, 85, 91, 96, 97, 105, 107, 108, 112, 113, 114, 121, 122, 123, 130, 131, 134, 135, 141, 144, 146, 151, 152, 156, 157, 162, 165, 167, 168, 169, 171, 172.

GLOSSARY

axil   The point where the leaf stalk joins the cane.

bareroot rose   A rose when dug from the nursery fields for sale.

basal shoot   A shoot coming from the crown of the bush.

bicolour   (Botanically spelled 'bicolor'.) A bloom with one side of the petals a colour distinctly different from that of the other.

blind shoot   A shoot which does not produce flowers.

bud   There are two types of bud. **1** One which will form a shoot, coming from a leaf axil. **2** One which will form a flower at the end of canes and laterals.

budding   Grafting a leaf-axil bud into the neck of a rootstock to propagate a rose.

budding union   The point where the bud has been inserted into the rootstock.

cane   A rose stem or shoot.

canker   A discolouration on a rose stem, caused by a wound, over which a callus forms.

climbing sport   A mutation in which a bush rose develops long canes and becomes a climber.

container-grown rose   A rose grown and sold in a container for immediate planting at any time of year.

crown   The point on a rose bush where the canes sprout from the rootstock.

die-back   A disease in which shoots turn brown, starting at the tip and working downwards. Caused by a fungus entering the plant tissue after mechanical damage or damage through frost.

disbudding   The removal of flower buds which are too close together to allow proper development of the remaining ones.

dormant A plant is dormant when growth is slowed down or ceases during periods of short days and low temperatures, i.e. in winter.

double Used of a rose with more than four rows of petals.

eye A dormant leaf-axil bud.

foliar feeding The spraying of liquid fertilizer on to leaves and canes, usually to supplement other fertilizers.

head The point where the canes of a standard rose grow from the budding union, at the top of the stem.

heading back The removal of canes from a rootstock after the rose which has been budded on to it has started to send out its own shoots.

heel When a shoot is pulled away from a cane to make cuttings, a heel of bark will be seen at the end.

heeling in The temporary planting of new roses in a trench to keep them fresh until the proper planting can be carried out.

hip The seed pod or fruit of the rose.

humus When organic matter decays a dark brown or black residue is left. This is humus and it improves soil texture and stimulates the bacterial activity necessary if plants are to flourish.

hybrid The crossing of two rose varieties or species, or a species and a variety, produces a hybrid.

lateral A side shoot growing from a main cane.

loam A rather loose term for a mixture of humus, sand and clay. The proportions can vary considerably.

mulch A top dressing put on the soil to add nutrients, stabilize its temperature and conserve moisture.

mutation See sport.

neck The part of the rootstock just above the roots. A bud is inserted in the neck in budding.

pegging down Bending over long rose canes and tying them down to pegs in the earth to encourage side shoots to break into growth.

pH scale Measures the acidity or alkalinity of soil.

8

pompon An old-style, rounded bloom with many short petals.

quartered bloom One in which the petals are infolded into four distinct sections. Found on many old roses.

raceme A long flower cluster, with blooms carried on flower stalks only, rather than side branches.

recurrent Blooming intermittently, with some flowers between the main flushes.

remontant Repeat-flowering.

rootstock A species rose, on to the roots of which a cultivated variety is budded. Also called understock or stock.

rugose With a wrinkled surface, used of leaves, as in the Rugosa roses.

scion The bud which is grafted on to a rootstock.

semi-double A rose with two or three rows of petals.

single A bloom having five petals only, but this term is sometimes used for one with up to about eight.

species **1** A group of plants differing minimally genetically. **2** A wild rose.

sport A form of mutation causing a shoot of a rose to bear flowers differing from those on the rest.

standard A rose variety budded on to a long-stemmed rootstock.

stock See rootstock.

sub-lateral A side shoot coming from a lateral.

sucker A cane growing from the rootstock.

systemic Chemical sprays which penetrate into the plant system and make it toxic.

truss A flower cluster as found on Floribundas.

understock See rootstock.

union See budding union.

variety A cultivated variety produced by hybridizing.

weeping standard A rambler or a climber, budded on to a tall stem so that the lax canes will hang down or 'weep' naturally and without training.

INTRODUCTION

The earliest fossil remains of what are almost certainly roses date from something like 35,000,000 years ago, long before there were men on the earth. However, from the time when man did progress from his early, primitive beginnings and began to appreciate the beauty in the world around him, the rose has been highly prized. It has figured in his art and literature, and in his heraldry. The Tudor Rose is just one of many of the forms which have been used in royal coats of arms, and the rose is, of course, the badge of England.

As a religious symbol of purity and goodness, the rose first came into prominence in pagan times. Later, the Christian Church frowned on it for this very reason, but gradually the Church adapted its thinking when it realized that people would not be denied what they had so long cherished. They wanted their roses, not only for their charm as flowers, but because over hundreds of years, and in fact until comparatively modern times, it was believed that the various parts of the rose had medicinal properties which would cure anything from madness to mumps. Vast fields of the earliest cultivated rose family, the Gallica or French Rose, were grown in France and elsewhere for the preparation of potions for every known ailment, and also for the making of conserves from their petals. It is said (though it may be one of the myths which abound in the history of the rose) that the Dog Rose was so called because the Romans believed that an infusion from its roots was a cure for hydrophobia.

From the very earliest days the rose has been grown for its perfume, for the production of Attar of Roses, which for centuries has been a major industry in the

Balkans, Turkey and neighbouring areas, but using the rose in the garden in the way we do today is of much more recent origin.

Though there have been roses in gardens since at least the time of one of the earliest rose lovers, Charlemagne, the rose garden as such was a much later creation. It was the wife of Napoleon, the Empress Josephine, who created what is considered to be the first, at her villa of Malmaison outside Paris. Following her example, the fashion spread to the chateaux of the nobility, and then to the big country houses of the British Isles and elsewhere. This continued to be the pattern for a long while, and it was not really until towards the end of the nineteenth century, with the founding of the National Rose Society (now the Royal National Rose Society), and the sudden interest in rose shows all over the United Kingdom, that people with smaller amounts of land and modest incomes realized that they, too, could have rose gardens. So began what can only be described as an avalanche of roses into every home. It has never ceased.

In this book there is a selection of garden roses which begins with some which probably go back to the time before recorded history, and includes the latest and best of the modern Hybrid Teas and Floribundas in all their multitudinous range of colours. Among the shrub roses, care has been taken to include many suitable for small plantings, but if a particular favourite among these or any of the other groups is not included, this is something difficult to avoid. Personal choice plays a big part in the creation of any garden, and there are well over 10,000 different roses to select from in cultivation all over the world at the present time.

In the pages where the varieties which are included are described and illustrated, such factors as resistance to disease, vigour, and the ultimate size to which they should grow (height followed by diameter) are mentioned. All three of these should be treated as a guide only. The situation in which a rose is grown, the type of soil, the part of the country, the care given in its cultivation, and the quality of the plant in the first place can all affect performance, sometimes to a surprising degree. Going to a reliable and specialist rose nursery will at least get things off to a good start.

The name of the rose, the name of the raiser and the date of introduction are given wherever possible, followed by the names of the two or more varieties which were cross-pollinated to produce it. The trial ground awards shown where appropriate are those which have been given after a three-year test period in the trial grounds at the Royal National Rose Society in England. A Gold Medal rose is something really outstanding, a Certificate of Merit is only a little lower, and a Trial Ground Certificate means that the rose is a very sound one for the average garden. The proportion of roses which get any award at all is quite small, so they are a select band, but not every raiser sends his new varieties for trial in the first place. These one can only judge from experience in growing them in the garden, and some have been included as they have proved to be roses of high quality. Those selected from about or before the turn of the century made their appearance before the award system was instituted, but have stood the test of time.

Now a word about the classification of roses into different groups, for we are losing the long familiar terms Hybrid Tea and Floribunda. There will be other changes as well, and all this comes about because roses are, through the interbreeding of one variety with another, and one family with another, losing their once clearly distinguishable characteristics. For instance, the flowers of many Floribundas are getting bigger, with fewer on a truss, and more and more they are developing the high-centred, Hybrid Tea type of bloom. In other groups, too, there has been confusion for a long time, and the World Federation of Rose Societies, to which the national societies are affiliated, has decided that it is more than time that things were sorted out. The adoption of its ideas by gardeners, and indeed by the nursery trade, will take time. It may be several years before they are generally accepted, so the old terms have been used for the main headings in this book. The alternative new ones are included in parentheses in each case.

The whole point of growing roses is that one should enjoy the most beautiful flowers there are, both in the garden and for decorating the house. Nothing else gives such value, for roses are very little trouble to look after, and incredibly tough and long-lived plants. The greatest heat roses are likely to encounter in Western Europe, even sustained over many weeks, does not seriously worry them, though it may cause the blooms to open quickly and possibly burn or fade the petals of some varieties. As long as roses are given plenty of water they will thrive, and all except the very tenderest (none of which is included in the following pages) will stand up to long periods of frost with, at the worst, the dying back of one or two canes. Properly looked after, rose bushes should last for twenty years at the very least. Some will go on for a great deal longer than this, and it is worth while taking some trouble to encourage them to do so.

The intention of this book is to show that nothing one has to do to keep roses in tip-top condition need be difficult or laborious, and that such things as pruning and propagation do not really hold any mysteries.

By bringing in a selection of the old and new shrub roses, it has been possible to give a much better picture of the full range of uses to which the rose can be put in the garden. There are varieties for bedding, for rockeries, for hedges of all heights, for shrubberies, for specimen planting, and for climbing up, over or through everything imaginable. There are even roses for ground cover, but the one place in which they will not grow is among the goldfish of a lily pond. But then, does one really want them to?

The flowers of the rose are infinitely variable, from the simple beauty of the five-petalled wild rose, through semi-doubles to the multitude of infolded petals of many of the old varieties. For a long time now the standard of rose perfection has been considered a Hybrid Tea with the centre petals whorled together into a high point and the rest reflexing outwards round them. This is the kind of bloom which wins medals on the show bench, and is certainly of unsurpassed loveliness. However, many, many roses do not grow naturally like this. If they have few petals, or if they have many but those in the centre of the flower are short, they may open cupped in shape, or form pompons, but this does not mean that they are any less beautiful. Each should be judged by its own standards.

The blooms of roses cover every colour of the spectrum with one exception. A number are made up of many colours, blended and shaded with great subtlety, and some change colour as the flower ages, often pleasingly as with the China roses, but not, it must be admitted, always so. But there are no blue roses.

Despite the fact that numbers of varieties have been called 'Blue This' and 'Blue That', none has, in fact, been other than deep lavender pink or mauve, and it seems most unlikely, except by a freak of nature – a natural mutation – that there ever will be a true blue. The chemical make-up of the genus *Rosa* lacks an essential ingredient, delphinidin (from which delphiniums take their name), and the cleverest hybridist cannot supply it. No one can say that they have not tried in every way they know to produce the blue rose, but strangely it is rare to talk to a gardener who will say that he really wants one.

No doubt if the miracle did happen, a blue variety

would sell in the same spectacular way that bright yellow, flame and orange garden roses did when they arrived on the scene for the first time at the beginning of this century. It would be, as they were, a novelty. It is not often remembered that that the first yellow roses for the garden were only put on the market in 1900 – the result of much patient crossing of a wild yellow Persian rose with other varieties over many years by a French nurseryman named Joseph Pernet-Ducher – and that our grandparents, great-grandparents, and all those who came before them, managed very happily with the white, pinks, mauves, maroons and reds of the old roses.

There was, as a matter of fact, an unfortunate side effect of the introduction of this Persian species, *R. foetida persiana*, into rose breeding lines. Before it came, black spot was certainly not unknown, but rose books published before the end of the nineteenth century scarcely mention it, so it can hardly have been a serious problem. The Persian rose, perhaps because it was now growing far from its native habitat, turned out to be particularly susceptible, and this susceptibility has been passed on. There are few Hybrid Teas or Floribundas nowadays that do not have at least some *R. foetida persiana* blood in their veins through interbreeding which has taken place over the last eighty years.

The story of how the modern rose developed is an incredibly complicated one, and perhaps the best way of showing it in its simplest form is in a family tree of the main species, varieties and groups. This is set out on p. 17, but it should be borne in mind that the early dates given are only very approximate. New families were developed only gradually, and no specific date can be put on the first variety in many instances. Hybrid Teas, for example, did not become a distinct group until long after the first one, 'La France', was bred in 1867. It was only when many other roses with similar general characteristics had been raised that it was decided to separate out the Hybrid Teas, and people then looked backwards to try to decide which was the earliest of them. Not surprisingly, there was, and still is, some dispute about which this was, but most now give the vote to 'La France'. In other old groups there has been even greater uncertainty.

Ramblers and climbers were developed from species such as *R. multiflora*, *R. wichuraiana*, *R. gigantea* and others from the Far East, first crossed naturally in the wild, and later by nurserymen with many other rose families.

Their origins are so mixed that it is quite impossible to make any general statement about the derivation of modern shrub roses. Some are simply extra-large Floribundas or Hybrid Teas, while others may have in their parentage (either directly or several generations removed) species, or any of the many rose families, old or new, including climbers and ramblers.

THE FAMILY TREE OF THE GARDEN ROSE

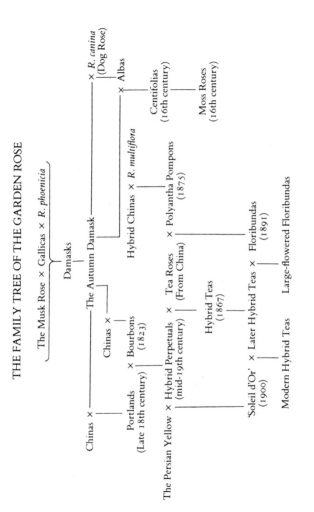

CULTIVATION

SOIL PREPARATION

The idea that roses grow best in clay is a myth. It arose many years ago when most roses were grown in the gardens of big country houses, where a full staff of gardeners was at hand to dig cart-loads of manure into the soil, which, in addition to supplying plant foods, both lightened it and improved the drainage. Roses must have a soil that is well drained and yet retains moisture and this, in gardens where there was water-retaining clay, is what such laborious treatment gave them. Probably as a result they did rather better than elsewhere, but it was not the clay on its own that did it.

A good medium loam to start with is the ideal, but if you are not lucky enough to have this already, some work will be needed to get the best results. Carry this out at least two months before the roses are due to arrive, to give the soil time to settle down again, and to give the humus you have added time to make a start on its gradual breaking down. Make sure that all perennial weeds are removed from the bed, particularly those with underground runners, otherwise you will be heading for trouble in the future.

The acidity of your soil is important, and soil-testing kits (with instructions for their use) are available from most garden shops and centres. They measure acidity in what is called a pH number. For roses this should be about 6.5, or slightly acid. Lime will increase alkalinity, but it is all too easy to overdo it, and once lime is in the soil it is difficult to get rid of. Nitro-chalk is the thing to use, and, for increasing acidity, peat.

Any type of soil, but particularly light, sandy ones, will benefit from the digging in of humus – well rotted

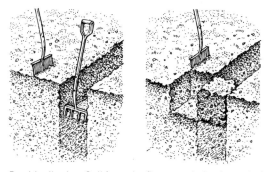

Double digging. Soil from the first trench dug is carried to the far end of the plot to fill in the last one. Plenty of humus-forming material takes its place at the bottom of each trench to improve drainage.

farmyard manure if you can get it, or well rotted compost. This, as was mentioned just now, helps to break up heavy ground, holds water, provides plant foods, and darkens the earth so that it absorbs and retains heat from the sun more easily. Peat does much the same but contains no nutrients, so a fertilizer must be used with it.

Double digging is nowadays only considered necessary on the very heaviest soils, mainly to improve drainage. If it has to be done on yours, dig manure, compost or coarse peat freely into the top spit, adding two or three handfuls of bone meal and hoof and horn meal per square metre (square yard). For light soils and medium ones, only the top spit need be dug over, with the same materials added.

Roses do not thrive on chalk with a thin layer of soil over it. If this is what you have, the chalk must be dug out to a depth of at least 45cm (18in), and plenty of peat (to increase acidity) must be added to the soil you replace it with.

It is unwise to dig up old roses from a rosebed and replace them with new ones, as these will never do well. The soil is likely to have become what is known as 'rose-sick', though other plants will be quite happy in it.

PLANTING

When buying roses it is best to get them from a nursery. If you order them in plenty of time to make sure of getting the varieties you want, they should arrive in good condition some time in late autumn, the best time for planting. The soil then will still be relatively warm and the roots can establish themselves before winter sets in. With pre-packed roses, select only those with a minimum of two healthy-looking, firm, unwrinkled green canes which are no thinner than a pencil. If storage temperatures have not been right in a shop or supermarket, polythene wrappings can cause all sorts of problems, from drying out to premature growth.

If frost or waterlogged ground prevents you planting your roses straight away, store them, unpacked, for up to a week or so, in a cool, frost-proof shed. If a longer delay is unavoidable, heel them in. This means unpacking them and burying them almost completely in a shallow trench, with at least 15cm (6in) of soil over the roots. There they can be left for five or six weeks, but do plant as soon as possible.

Whether heeling in or planting, inspect the roses after unpacking. Damaged or diseased canes should be cut back cleanly to a healthy-looking bud. Trim back long, thick roots, by about two-thirds and snip off any remaining leaves. Should the plants look dry, put them in a bucket of water for at least an hour. While they are soaking, prepare a planting mixture, approximately half a bucketful per rose, of equal parts of soil and granulated peat, with a handful per plant of bone meal well mixed in.

Planting holes should be dug large enough for the

20

roots of bareroot roses to be well spread out, and deep
enough for the budding union (the point where the
canes sprout from the roots) to be just below soil level.
Put the first rose into its hole, spread the roots evenly all
round, and check with a cane across the hole that the

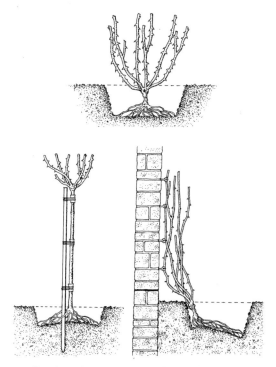

Planting a bush rose, a standard and a climber.

depth is right. If it is, hold the bush upright, tip planting mixture over the roots from a bucket, tread this gently, and then rake in on top of it the soil dug from the hole. Tread once more, firmly but not too heavily, and then top up with more soil.

Plant climbing roses at least 45cm (18in) away from a wall, near which the earth will usually be very dry. Lean the bushes in towards the wall, with the roots fanning outwards towards moister ground.

Container-grown roses should have full-sized planting holes so that the roots can penetrate the loosened earth round them easily. A hole little bigger than the container may simply form a sump in which water will gather and do the rose no good.

With standard roses, drive the stake in before planting to avoid damaging the roots. Do not plant too deeply, which will encourage suckers, and leave the ties quite loose for a few weeks until the soil has settled down and the rose with it. Otherwise the rose might be left suspended too near the surface.

TRAINING CLIMBERS AND RAMBLERS

It would be as well first of all to explain the difference between the two, something often found confusing. Most ramblers, such as 'Crimson Shower', are descended from a species rose called *R. wichuraiana*, from which they inherit their huge trusses of small flowers, which come once a year only. New canes which grow up from the base each year bear the best flowers the following summer. A smaller group of ramblers, of which the old favourite 'Albertine' is an example, come from *R. luciae*, a close relative of *R. wichuraiana*. Their new canes tend to branch out from higher up, the flowers come rather earlier (though still only once a year), and are rather bigger.

Climbers have bigger flowers still, in smaller trusses, sometimes of only three or four, and they make a more

22

or less permanent framework of their main canes. Many, like 'Danse du Feu', are recurrent.

The first and most obvious reason for training both climbers and ramblers is to keep them under control and to make them grow where they are wanted. The second is to make sure that plenty of flowers are produced low down, and not just at the top. If the canes are simply allowed to go straight up, the sap has an uninterrupted flow along them. It will bypass most of the side buds and only those at the tips of the canes will grow and produce flowers. If, however, the canes are trained as horizontally as possible the sap flow is restricted and sap flows out into the side buds as well, so that they form side shoots or laterals, which bear leaves and bloom. These laterals, in their turn, will branch out, so that gradually the climber moves upwards to cover a wall or pergola.

On such a wall, or on a close-boarded fence, the easiest way to train climbers is on strong, galvanized iron wires. These should run horizontally across the wall about 45cm (18in) apart and not less than 8cm (3in) from the surface. They can be strung between vine eyes driven into the wall, which is made easier if a hole slightly smaller than the vine eye is first drilled in the brickwork. On a wooden fence, this preliminary drilling is not, of course, necessary. The reason that the wires are set out from the wall is to allow for proper air circulation round the rose canes, which will help to prevent fungus diseases like mildew and black spot. Even with this precaution, as ramblers are particularly prone to mildew, it is best to keep them away from walls altogether, though they can be grown on a trellis-type, openwork fence.

Once the wires are up, the climber can be fanned out and the canes trained along them, tying them in with plastic covered garden wire to the outside of the wires on the wall. Do not tuck them in behind them, because when pruning time comes along anything that has to be cut away will be difficult to disentangle.

Training climbers and ramblers. Avoid walls for ramblers; use horizontal wires between wooden uprights.

Either climbers or ramblers on individual pillars, or on the uprights of a pergola or arch, should be trained in a spiral round them, rather than straight up. Horizontal training here is impossible, and this is the next best way of encouraging the side shoots to break.

In dealing with ramblers, try to train them so that the main canes do not become too entwined with each other. When pruning is described (p. 26), it will be seen that the canes which have flowered should be removed each year, and if they are inextricably mixed up this becomes a major problem.

FERTILIZERS

Roses are plants which like plenty of nourishment and, especially on light soils, many of the chemical salts on which they feed will, after a time, be used up or washed away by rain. A well-fed rose, in addition to having the best flowers, will have a much greater resistance to disease.

The most important ingredients of a rose fertilizer are nitrogen to stimulate growth, phosphates for the roots and flowers, potash for resistance to drought and disease and for good growth generally, and there are also a number of others in smaller quantities. If the quantities are really minute, they are known as trace elements, but these are important, nonetheless.

The table shows the proportions needed for mixing a fertilizer, but unless a very large number of roses is grown, it will be easier to buy a proprietary mixture, which will have all the ingredients in exactly the right proportions. Always use gloves when handling fertilizers.

Immediately after pruning, and when the soil is damp, sprinkle a small handful of fertilizer round each rose and hoe it in lightly. Repeat in midsummer after the first flush of bloom, but no later. Otherwise soft late autumn growth is encouraged, which frost may damage or kill. However, sulphate of potash at the rate of 56g per m² (2oz per square yard), put on in August, will help to ripen late canes.

Foliar feeds can also be purchased. These are sprayed on to the leaves and are absorbed direct into the plant's system, bypassing the roots. They can have advantages in alkaline soils, in which the roots have difficulties in taking up iron, but in general they are best as a supplement to other fertilizers, which act more slowly and last longer.

A good, general-purpose rose fertilizer

Sulphate of magnesium	1 part
Sulphate of iron	1 part
Sulphate of ammonia	2½ parts
Sulphate of potash	5 parts
Superphosphate of lime	8 parts

PRUNING

This is something generally approached with a greater degree of trepidation than almost any other aspect of gardening, and the reason must surely be that, when it is described in words, pruning does sound incredibly complicated. It is, in fact, a perfectly simple and logical operation and quickly carried out, provided, and this is the important point, the *reason* for pruning is fully understood. Once one knows this, the actual operation becomes quite straightforward.

In nature, in the hedgerows, a rose sends up new canes each year from somewhere near ground level. The following summer these bear the best flowers, but from that time on they will begin to deteriorate. The following summer they and their flowers will not be of the same quality, the canes may have become diseased, and gradually over a number of seasons they will die away. But new canes will have scrambled up through the undergrowth to replace them.

Roses in our gardens grow in exactly the same way, and pruning is simply a way of getting rid of the old growth more quickly, and encouraging more and better healthy new wood.

There are, however, two other reasons for pruning. One is to build up a reasonably balanced bush, and the other is to thin out tangled growth in the centre to allow a good circulation of air.

Having established the basic principles, it would seem to follow that all roses should be pruned in the same way, but all of them are not the same. With Hybrid Teas, for instance, the size and quality of their comparatively few large flowers is all-important, and the maximum amount of strong new wood is needed to produce them, so that they are pruned harder than any other kind of rose. Most other types, and this includes Floribundas, are grown for the mass of smaller blooms they carry, and the size and quality of each flower is not

26

so vital. Pruning can therefore be lighter and the replacement of the main canes more gradual.

Pruning is done with secateurs, which should always be kept clean and sharp. Buy a good pair, which will last a lifetime. Some of the cheaper ones on the market can, when cutting, bruise a stem badly below the cut and encourage the entry of disease. Cuts should be made about 6mm (¼in) above a bud, sloping down away from it at an angle of about 45°. Cutting to an outward-facing bud will encourage growth away from the centre of the bush, but if the rose is a lax, sprawling grower it is better to cut to an inward-facing one in the hope that the rose will gain height. It may well be, however, that it is another, lower, bud which springs into growth in due course, in which case the stump left above it should be trimmed off later to avoid it dying back. If the centre of any cane you cut is brown and discoloured, this means that die-back is already spreading down the shoot. Cut to a lower bud and continue to do so until clean white wood is reached. For more about die-back, see p. 37.

Provided one is not in the middle of a frosty spell, the traditional time for pruning is very early spring. In the colder areas it is probably better to wait until a little later, but the time to do it is when the buds are just showing signs of breaking into growth, but before they have actually put out leaves. Waiting until this happens wastes a great deal of the plant's energy. These times are, as I have said, traditional, but in actual fact pruning can take place at any period when the roses are dormant, even in early winter. However, such early treatment can mean frost damage to the pruned canes and another going over in the spring.

New roses planted in the autumn should be pruned really hard in the spring, except in the case of ramblers and climbers, which should be left as they are received from the nursery. The canes of all others should be reduced to no more than 10cm (3–4in) long, which may

27

seem exceptionally drastic but pays in the long run. It means that top-growth starts slowly and that the rose's initial energy goes into developing a good root system, which is like putting down sound foundations for a house. Roses planted in the spring should be pruned in the same way at the time of planting.

Hybrid Teas Prune away all weak and diseased shoots, leaving only those which look at least as thick as a pencil. Remove thick stumps left from previous prunings (even if they are still green) from which no strong new canes have sprouted. In some cases a fine-toothed pruning saw may be needed for this. Thin out the centre of the bush if it is getting cluttered. If two canes are crossing so that they rub together, remove one of them. Cut the canes which are left to about 20–25cm

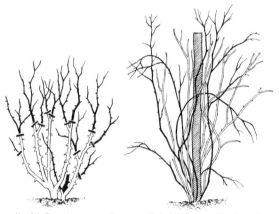

(Left) Pruning a bush rose: Hybrid Tea or Floribunda. (Right) Pruning a rambler. Normally this would be done with the rose in full leaf, but leaves are not shown for clarity. Shoots to be removed are shaded black.

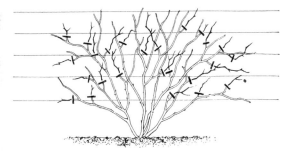

Pruning a climber. Only the laterals are shortened.

(8–10in). Cut to the bud nearest to these limits, but do not worry if it is a little outside them. This is called medium pruning and will suit most gardens. Harder pruning will produce bigger flowers and probably less of them. Lighter pruning will result in more and smaller flowers. Very strong Hybrid Teas like 'Peace' do better with not too much being removed. Leave them 45–60cm (18–24in) high.

Floribundas Follow the same procedure, with the main canes ending up 30–35cm (12–14in) in length and cutting back strong side shoots by about two-thirds.

Climbing Roses If these are climbing sports of bush varieties (always prefixed by the word 'Climbing', e.g. 'Climbing Masquerade') do not prune in their first year as this may cause reversion to their bush form. Subsequently, simply cut back side shoots or laterals to one or two eyes (buds) from the main canes. If bare at the base after some years, cut a main cane hard back to encourage new growth low down.

Ramblers After flowering, cut right to ground level all canes which have bloomed, and tie the newly formed

Pruning a shrub rose. Only the laterals are shortened.

canes in their place. In years when the latter are scanty, leave a few of the old canes, only trimming back the laterals as with climbers. The old canes produce some flowers. With ramblers of the 'Albertine' group, cut away old, flowered growth just above the point where a vigorous new cane has sprouted from it.

Standards   Most of these will be of Hybrid Tea or Floribunda varieties, and the same general sequence should be followed for them. Pay particular attention to the balance of the head. Weeping Standards are formed from ramblers (the long, flexible canes of which hang down and 'weep' naturally), and less frequently from climbers. Pruning should be as described for both these classes.

Miniatures   These need little pruning except for a light trim to keep them tidy, and the occasional thinning out of those varieties which form a thick tangle of twigs.

Shrub Roses   To increase the flower production of most of these, cut back side shoots by about two-thirds to a bud. Do this after flowering with the non-recurrent kinds. Otherwise simply remove dead or diseased wood as and when it occurs. Species roses require no pruning at all, but dead wood should be taken away.

DEAD-HEADING

Once a flower has been fertilized, it produces seeds. In the case of a rose, these are contained in the hips, which form as the flowers fade and die. If they are left on the bush, a great deal of energy will go into their development, rather than into the production of new flowers. If they are removed before they can swell and grow, the rose will try again, and the result will be another flush of bloom on the bush.

The spent flowers should not, however, simply be pulled off, or one will be left with unsightly flower stalks and, in the case of Floribundas, a flowerless truss. Cut the cane which has borne flowers just above the second or third bud down. This will ensure a stronger new shoot developing. Do not remove hips which are grown for decoration on once-flowering old roses.

Dead heading. Cut to a leaf-axil bud 10-12cm (4-5in) below the old flower head.

SUCKERS

Almost all roses are bud-grafted on to a rootstock, which is the root of a wild rose. This gives them greater vigour and other good qualities. A sucker is a growth coming from the rootstock, and if it is not removed, the roots will put all their energy into the sucker rather than into the variety which is budded on to it. Never cut a sucker, which will be the equivalent of pruning it and will simply encourage more suckers. Pull the sucker off at the point at which it joins the roots, and no more will form from the same point. Usually the leaves, thorns and the colour of the wood of a newly-formed sucker will be very different from those of the true rose. There are often, though not always, seven leaflets to each leaf, as opposed to five leaflets on a cultivated variety. If in any doubt, trace a suspected sucker back to its source, even if this means scraping some soil away from the roots to find it. If it is a sucker, pull smartly.

Tracing and removing a sucker.

DISEASES AND PESTS

Liquid chemical sprays are the easiest and most effective way of dealing with both of these. Dusting with chemical powders is only really practical if the number of roses to be dealt with is very small, and even then it is difficult to give complete coverage of the leaves and stems, which is essential if the powder is to work properly. Systemic liquid sprays enter a plant's system, making the sap toxic and, as they cannot be washed off by rain, they will remain active for several weeks, no matter what the weather is like. Spraying with them can be done less often, an important consideration with the ever-increasing price of chemicals.

However, a number of people do not like using chemical sprays, and there are less harmful (non-systemic) products on the market which derive from natural sources. Generally speaking they will not be as long-lasting in their effects or anything like as active against diseases, but whatever you do decide to use, do not spray unless you have to or you will be wasting both time and money. The most common insect pests of roses are aphids or greenfly, but in some seasons they may hardly be seen at all, or may vanish very quickly if they do come. Again, the two commonest diseases, black spot and mildew, are almost equally unpredictable, and the intensity of the attack can vary greatly from district to district. So the best rule to follow is to wait for the very first sign of a disease or pest and then to spray promptly. Only experience in your own area will tell you how often the spraying has to be repeated. When carrying it out, which should not be done in the heat of the day, make sure that the under sides of the leaves as well as the tops are wetted.

The charts on p 36 and p 38 show the basic chemical constituent of the best sprays for various purposes. This will also be given on the packet or bottle of a proprietary fungicide or insecticide, together with instructions for mixing, which should be followed exactly. Experience has shown that it is best to vary the type of spray from year to year, as both insects and diseases quite rapidly build up an immunity if only one kind is used. It must be added, too, that while mildew and most insects can nowadays be quite simply dealt with, there is no really effective remedy for black spot. It is only possible to achieve some degree of control.

Diseases

Black spot Round black spots with fringed edges, usually appearing first on the older, lower leaves from midsummer onwards. If left unchecked, it will spread rapidly up the bush and on to others by means of airborne spores. The spots increase in size and the leaves eventually turn yellow and drop off. Loss of their food-manufacturing leaves weakens the plants, and bad attacks of black spot over a number of years may kill them. Remove and burn affected leaves and spray promptly. Clean all infected leaves from the beds in late autumn, and burn them, too. One or two winter sprays of dormant bushes with Jeyes Fluid or Bordeaux mixture (diluted according to the instructions on the bottle) may help to kill over-wintering spores of both mildew and black spot and insect eggs as well.

Mildew First seen, at any time from mid-spring onwards, as small, greyish, powdery-looking spots on the leaves and the flower stalks. It will quickly spread to the whole plant and on to others nearby, again by airborne spores. Mildew is not fatal, but a bad attack is very unsightly and can distort and retard growth, sometimes preventing flower buds from opening properly. Spray when the first signs are seen.

Rust Usually this is only prevalent in certain districts, and then on certain varieties only. Small orange pustules under the leaves, which darken as they age, are the first signs, and rust must be dealt with at once, as it can be a killer. Plantvax spray is, fortunately, completely effective.

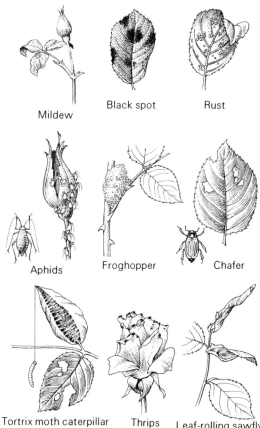

Mildew

Black spot

Rust

Aphids

Froghopper

Chafer

Tortrix moth caterpillar   Thrips   Leaf-rolling sawfly

Diseases and pests.

Rose Fungicides

Proprietary name	Black Spot	Mildew	Rust	Active Ingredient
Benlate	★★★	★★★	–	Benomyl
Dithane	★★	–	★★	Zineb
Dithane (2)	★★	–	★★	Mancozeb
Saprol	★★★	★★★	–	Triforine
ICI Garden Fungicide	★★	–	★★	Thiram
Karathane, Crotothane	–	★★	–	Dinocap
Maneb w.p.	★★	–	★★	Maneb
Mildothane	★★★	★★★	–	Thiophanate-methyl
Nimrod-T	★★★	★★★	–	Bupirimate-triforine
Bayleton	★★	★★★	–	Triadimefon
EL. 222, Rubigan	★★★	★★★	★	Fenarimol
Plantvax	–	–	★★★	Oxycarboxin

★★★ Very active   ★★ Moderately active   ★ Some effect

Die-back   Shoots turn brown and die from the top downwards. It is caused by the entry of a fungus into damaged wood, canker or by lack of soil chemicals, particularly potash which helps ripening. Frost damage on unripened canes can cause die-back. Cut the affected shoot away to the first healthy bud.

Insect Pests

Aphids   Very small green and sometimes brown insects in clusters on young shoots, leaves and flower stems suck the sap; a bad attack will stunt growth.

Froghoppers   Small and greenish-yellow insects, hiding in blobs of white foam often in a leaf axil. Wash away foam before spraying.

Chafers   Large brown flying beetles which nibble the petals and anthers. The large white grubs attack rose roots, and in a bad attack the soil should be disinfected.

Tortrix moth and other caterpillars   The signs are holes eaten in the leaves, and holes bored in flower buds. Pick off caterpillars by hand or, in a bad attack, spray. Some caterpillars, including those of the lackey moth, make small, web-like structures, or else can be found inside rolled-up leaves. Pinch, pick off, and burn.

Leaf-rolling sawfly   Most often found in gardens sheltered by trees, where the air is comparatively still. The eggs are laid in the leaf margins, and the leaf rolls up to protect the grub. Preventive spraying early in the season is the only remedy, as it will not be effective once the leaves have curled. If this has happened, the leaves must be pulled off to prevent grubs dropping to lower ones and spreading the trouble.

Thrips   Tiny, brownish-yellow insects which nibble flower buds, particularly of the paler varieties. They thrive especially in hot weather.

Rose Insecticides

Proprietary names have not been listed as there are numerous competing brands.

Active ingredient	Caterpillars, chafers	Leaf-rolling sawfly	Aphids, froghoppers	Thrips
Dimethoate or formothion	*	—	***	*
Malathion or diazinon	*	—	**	*
Menazon	—	—	***	—
Gamma BHC (HCH)	*	aggravates attack	*	*
Trichlorphon	**	**	—	—
Fenitrothion	**	*	**	*

*** Very active   ** Moderately active   * Some effect

The charts for both the fungicides and the insecticides are based on information compiled by the Scientific Adviser to the Royal National Rose Society.

Taking cuttings

Most roses, with the noticeable exception of Hybrid Teas, take quite readily from cuttings. Particularly easy to root are climbers and ramblers, miniatures and the majority of shrub roses. Floribundas are reasonably easy, some more than others.

At any time between late summer and early winter

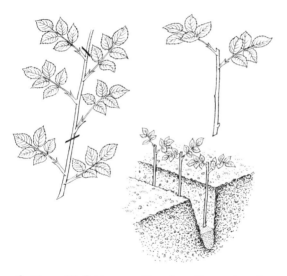

Cuttings. (1) Taking a cutting from the centre of a shoot. (2) A cutting with a bud at the bottom and all but the top pair of leaves removed. (3) Planting cuttings in a 15cm (6in) deep trench, with a sprinkling of coarse sand at the bottom.

(though not in a heatwave) choose a corner of the garden which gets plenty of light but is shaded from the midday sun. Dig a narrow slit trench 15cm (6in) deep, with one side vertical. Sprinkle coarse sand along the bottom, which will encourage rooting. For the cuttings, use shoots which have flowered, as these should have reached the right degree of ripeness. From the centre of the first of these, cut 23cm (9in) lengths, making the cuts just below and just above a leaf. Leave the top pair of leaves on each cutting, removing the rest and the thorns. Moisten the bottoms, and dip them into a hormone rooting powder, next placing each, upright and 15cm (6in) apart, in the trench against the vertical side. Fill in

Budding. (1) Making the 'T' cut. (2) Cutting the bud or scion. (3) Inserting the bud in the rootstock. (4) Binding the bud in place.

and firm the soil, firming again after frost. The cuttings should be ready for planting out the following autumn.

Budding or bud-grafting
Under the heading Suckers (p. 32) it was mentioned that roses are budded or bud-grafted on to rootstocks. A local rose nursery may agree to supply rootstocks if only a few are wanted, but otherwise there are suppliers who specialize in them and who advertise in the gardening press. Stocks grown from wild rose cuttings can be used, but are very variable in performance. Plant rootstocks in autumn, and by the following summer they should be ready for budding. Wait for humid, showery weather before you begin. A proper budding knife or a razor-sharp penknife will be the only tool needed.

Scrape soil away from the neck of a stock and wipe it clean with a damp rag. About 5cm (2in) up the neck from the roots, make a horizontal cut about 1cm ($\frac{1}{2}$in) long, just penetrating the bark but no deeper. From the centre of this, make another similar but downwards cut about 3cm (1$\frac{1}{4}$in) long, so that the two cuts form a 'T'.

Cut a strong, healthy shoot from the rose you wish to bud. One shoot of reasonable size should provide 3–4 buds from the centre portion. Snip off the leaves, leaving the leaf stalks, and with your knife, using a scooping action, cut out the first bud. Start about 1cm ($\frac{1}{2}$in) above it, and come out about 1cm below. You now have what is known as the scion, and the sliver of wood under the bark should be eased out with a thumbnail.

Placing the bud in a safe place, with the blunter reverse end of your budding knife, ease out the triangular flaps of bark enclosed within the arms of the 'T' cut in the rootstock. Be careful not to cut or tear them. Hold the scion by its leaf stalk, and ease it right down under the flaps. Secure it in place with a budding tie, or bind firmly but not too tightly with raffia.

Provided the bud takes, a shoot should form from it

in due course, the beginnings of your new rose. Wind could blow this out of the stock in its early stages, so support it by tying to a cane driven into the ground. In spring, cut away the top-growth of the rootstock.

Standard roses, if the stock is from the species *R. rugosa*, should have two buds, staggered, inserted into the top of the stem. If the stock comes from *R. canina*, insert them into two side shoots, as close to the stem as possible.

THE ROSE FAMILIES

'Canary Bird'   Daffodil yellow
Probably a hybrid of *R. xanthina*. From Northern China and Korea.

If you grow this it is likely to be the first rose to bloom in your garden, opening its buds in an exceptional year in the middle of spring. At other times it will be in full flower by the end of the spring and will carry on well into summer, lasting four to five weeks, though there will be no repeat later. The flowers, which are slightly scented, are carried all along the arching canes, and are about the brightest and largest of all the spring-flowering yellow roses.

The bush will eventually be a big one, probably about 210cm × 210cm (7ft × 7ft), but 'Canary Bird' makes a very effective standard and is quite easily obtainable in this form, in which it will be much more restrained and quite suitable for a small garden. The dainty, fern-like foliage is always attractive and healthy.

R. moyesii   Bright scarlet
From western China about 1894.

The picture this time is of the hips rather than the flowers
in order to show that many species, though they only
have one flowering period, can put on a second and
different kind of display in later summer and autumn.
This is particularly so of *R. moyesii* and its many hybrids,
such as 'Geranium', 'Sealing Wax' and 'Fred Streeter', in
which the hips are fully 5cm (2in) long and hang in
clusters like decorations on a Christmas tree for months
on end. *R. moyesii* itself is a 360cm × 300cm (12ft ×
10ft), open-growing shrub with healthy, dark green
leaves and spangled with single scarlet flowers with
creamy stamens but no scent. The flowers open in early
summer and will last a month or more. 'Geranium' is the
form generally recommended for the smaller garden,
but as it is only about 60cm (2ft) smaller each way than
the species it still needs a good deal of space. 'Fred Streeter'
is actually smaller still, the flowers cerise-pink.

45

_R._ × _paulii rosea_   Pale pink with lighter centre
Prior to 1903. _R. arvensis_ × a Rugosa.

This, and _R._ × _paulii_ itself, which has white flowers
instead of pink but is otherwise similar, is ideal for
covering large areas of waste ground, or for planting at
the front of a big shrub border. It will not often top
120cm (4ft), but may well spread out its long, fiercely
thorned canes to cover a circle of up to 4.5m (15ft),
making a dense, low thicket which will smother all
weeds. The leaves are attractive and grey-green, wrinkled, or rugose, in the style of one of the parents. It is
midsummer flowering, the multitudes of blooms, each
fully 75mm (3in) across, almost hiding the foliage from
sight. There is a rich scent with a hint of cloves about it.
_R._ × 'Macrantha' var. 'Raubritter' is another rose which
grows in the same kind of way and can be used for the
same purpose, though it will also climb. It will cover a
180cm (6ft) circle, and the clear pink, semi-double
blooms, which are borne in clusters, keep their globular
shape throughout. All three roses are healthy.

***R. spinosissima* 'Double Yellow'**   Daffodil yellow
Introduced about 1828. One of the Scots Briers or
Burnet Roses.

This is an early-flowering family of roses, all of them of
small stature, very prickly, and liable to spread by
underground suckers, which must be borne in mind
when planting. 'Double Yellow' makes a 150cm (5ft)
bush, will come into flower in late spring or early
summer, the informally shaped double blooms having a
bunch of green carpels in the centre and being strongly
scented. The flowers are followed by black hips like
large currants. It has the same type of small, fern-like
foliage as 'Canary Bird' and it is equally healthy. Like all
Spinosissimas it will thrive on dry sandy soils, where not
much else will grow.

'Double White' grows to about the same size, as
'Double Yellow', with clusters of globular blooms with
a lily-of-the-valley scent, 'Bicolor', which is lilac-pink
with a lighter reverse, reaches only 90cm (3ft), as does
'William III', which makes a crimson-purple mound.

GALLICAS (Old Garden Roses – Gallicas)

'Empress Josephine' (also called 'Francofurtana')

Deep pink
R. gallica × *R. cinnamomea*. From the late sixteenth century.

The Empress Josephine created what is generally considered to be the world's first rose garden at Malmaison outside Paris. This rose is dedicated to her, though it is unlikely that she actually grew it among her vast collection. It is an example of a Gallica more lax and spreading in habit than 'Rosa Mundi', and while it will reach 90–120cm (3–4ft) in height, its almost thornless canes will spread out to 120–150cm (4–5ft) all round, and are well branched. Flowering is from early summer to midsummer, with no repeat, but the rather loosely formed blooms make a fine display. The clear pink has a deeper veining. Less strongly scented than most Gallicas, but the leaves are better and less rough than many others. Some mildew is possible.

'Cardinal de Richelieu' is another Gallica of similar size and habit, with clusters of double blooms of a rich, deep maroon-purple.

'Rosa Mundi'   Blush pink, striped deep pink
R. gallica versicolor. Known since the sixteenth century.

The Gallicas are the oldest cultivated roses, and 'Rosa Mundi' is certainly of great antiquity. It is a sport of the even older 'Officinalis' (probably the Red Rose of Lancaster), the flowers of which are deep pink instead of being striped, and both make upright, compact, 120cm × 120cm (4ft × 4ft) shrubs. If you do not mind one crop of bloom only, they can be used for bedding. Otherwise they can go at the front of a planting of other shrubs or be used for a low hedge, when their slender, wiry canes have the advantage that they can be clipped over gently in winter instead of being pruned conventionally. Black spot will be rare, but the rather rough, typically Gallica leaves will certainly be attacked by mildew, and may discolour with age. All Gallicas sucker freely, and if on their own roots can be increased by rooted offsets (i.e. suckers which have formed their own roots). 'Rosa Mundi' is a gay novelty.

'Mme Hardy' White

Hardy, 1832. Possibly a Damask × Centifolia hybrid.

Probably the most beautiful white rose among the old varieties, the flat double blooms opening from pink-tinted buds to show a tiny green pointel at the heart of each. They are very fragrant, and are borne in large clusters on a strong-growing, well-branched shrub, which will reach about 180cm × 150cm (6ft × 5ft). It makes a fine specimen or is ideal for a mixed planting, with plentiful medium green leaves, which are slightly wrinkled and generally healthy, though mildew is not unknown. Early summer to midsummer flowering.

The earlier Damasks, among other roses, have been grown in the Balkans and neighbouring areas over the centuries for the production of Attar of Roses. Among the best of these for the garden is 'Ispahan', which is in flower longer than any other Damask. The strong, branching, 150cm × 120cm (5ft × 4ft) bush carries clusters of fragrant, clear pink, double blooms. Few thorns.

'St Nicholas'   Deep pink

This rose originated in a Yorkshire garden in 1950, but
whether it was a discovery of an old and forgotten
variety or whether it was an accidental modern hybrid
with some other Damask seems uncertain. It is a fairly
lax but quite compact grower, about 120cm × 120cm
(4ft × 4ft), which will make an admirable hedge, or can,
of course, be used as a specimen shrub. It is non-recurrent,
but is extremely free-flowering, coming into bloom in
early summer and lasting for many weeks. The semi-
double flowers with their yellow stamens are followed
by long-lasting red hips. The foliage is good and
generally healthy.

The 'Autumn Damask' or 'Four Seasons Rose', dating
from pre-Roman times, is an interesting one for any
collection, as it was the only rose from the West to be
recurrent before the China roses were introduced in the
eighteenth century. A 120cm × 90cm (4ft × 3ft) shrub,
its pink flowers are not, however, of the top quality.

ALBAS (Old Garden Roses – Albas)

'Königin von Dänemark' Pale pink, deeper in centre.
Booth, 1826.

Despite their name, only the two Albas discussed on the
next page are white. In the main they are in shades of
pink, as this one is, though such a brief description does
not do its colour justice. The flowers come in clusters in
early summer, a scarlet-pink at first, which is unique
among the old roses, and then lighten in tone as the
blooms open, though the stronger colour is still held in
the centre. By this time they are reflexed and quartered,
with a delicious fragrance

More lax and open in habit than most Albas, it will
reach about 150cm × 120cm (5ft × 4ft), but it retains the
family's grey-green leaves, which seem completely
healthy. A pearl among the old roses. 'Félicité Parmentier'
is another Alba of quite similar habit, if anything slightly
smaller, the buds being at first a pale primrose yellow
before opening to blush-pink flowers.

R. × *alba semi-plena* — White

Certainly this rose is very ancient and may have been brought to England by the Romans. It is quite possibly the White Rose of York, and the double-flowered form, R. × *alba maxima*, is thought to be the Jacobite rose of Bonnie Prince Charlie. True or not, both have become naturalized in certain areas of the north of England.

Both roses are very strong, upright growers, reaching 180cm × 150cm (6ft × 5ft), and one of the attractions of these and other Albas is the foliage, which is a grey-green. With it, they still keep attractive after the flowers, which come in the first two months of summer, have gone. It also makes a good foil for other leaf colours in a general shrub planting, for which R. × *alba semi-plena* is particularly suitable. There can be some spread by underground suckers, which must be allowed for. Red hips follow the flowers in substantial bunches. Generally very healthy.

53

'Fantin Latour'	Blush pink, fading lighter

Named after the famous French flower painter, this rose is a good deal more erect and upright in growth than the average Centifolia. More normally they have long lax canes, often borne down by the weight of the large, globular blooms, so that the support of stakes or a pillar may be necessary. 'Fantin Latour's' canes are reasonably rigid, so that it is able to display its breathtakingly beautiful bloom to great advantage all over the bush. It will probably reach 180cm × 150cm (6ft × 5ft), and has large, drooping leaves, which in this case are typical of the family. They may well need spraying against mildew, but black spot is unlikely. Fragrance is there, but it is not strong. Use as a specimen or in a shrub rose border, remembering that the flowering period is only from early to midsummer. Centifolias are the original cabbage roses, and go back to the early eighteenth century.

'Henri Martin' (also called 'Red Moss')

Scarlet-crimson

Laffay, 1863.

Because of the large number of their closely-packed petals, the Centifolia roses are unable to set seed, so that new varieties, mainly developed by the Dutch, were all sports. Some time in the sixteenth century a sport appeared, *R. × centifolia muscosa* or the 'Common Moss', which had a glandular, mossy growth on the flower stalks and sepals, and from this other Moss roses have sported over the years. Sometimes the moss is green and sometimes brownish, but the habit of all varieties is typically Centifolia, except in one or two cases where they are partially recurrent.

'Henri Martin' is the only scarlet-crimson Moss rose, and carries its clusters of flowers gracefully on a strong-growing 150cm × 120cm (5ft × 4ft) bush. The petals are unusually broad and neatly arranged in the bloom. The moss is green. Healthy.

'Petite de Hollande'   Soft pink

This is a typical Centifolia in every way, except in the
size of its flowers. They are quite small and so do not
weigh down the canes too much, enabling the bush to
keep reasonably compact and making it one of the best
to choose for a small garden. Globular in shape, the
flowers appear first in early summer and will keep on
well into the middle of the season, hanging in pendulous
clusters of five or six. About 120cm × 90cm (4ft × 3ft)
is the average size to which the bush will grow, with the
large leaves common to the type, which will not be
proof against mildew, though black spot is rare.

    R. × centifolia itself is known as 'Rose des Peintres',
and has huge, globular, deep-centred, pale pink flowers,
of the kind depicted by many of the old Dutch Masters.
Nobody quite knows where the Centifolias came from,
but they were largely developed in Holland.

RUGOSAS (Shrub Roses – Recurrent)
'Frau Dagmar Hastrup' (also called 'Frau Dagmar Hartopp')   Pale pink, lighter in centre

The Rugosa is the Ramanus Rose of Japan, though the family originated in parts of China as well.

Only those Rugosas with single flowers and a few of the semi-doubles have hips, but what spectacular ones they are, like small red tomatoes about 24mm (1in) in diameter. They appear on the bushes after the first crop of blooms, so that with the second crop flowers and hips are there together. 'Frau Dagmar' has some of the finest and largest hips of all.

There is another advantage with this rose, too, apart from its lovely, cream-stamened flowers, in that it does not grow too big, perhaps reaching 150cm × 120cm (5ft × 4ft), erect and sturdy, with plenty of completely healthy, wrinkled (rugose) leaves. Any soil suits. 'Pink Grootendorst' is a taller, more open-growing variety, with clusters of small, pink flowers, the petal edges frilled like a Dianthus.

'Roseraie de l'Hay'   Wine red
Cochet-Cochet, 1901. A *R. rugosa rosea* sport.

'Roseraie de l'Hay' makes a big, very bushy shrub, densely covered, right to the ground, with bright green, rugose leaves on which never a sign of disease is seen, and which take on yellow tints in the autumn before they fall.

The loosely-formed flowers really do come continuously in small clusters right through the summer and are very sweetly scented. They stand rain reasonably well, but are not long-lasting when cut. In any case cutting is never easy, for all the canes have an incredible number of needle-sharp prickles. This alone makes the rose an intruder-proof candidate for hedges, but its habit of growth is ideal as well. It will reach 180cm × 150cm (6ft × 5ft), so close planting is not needed.

Any soil will suit it, even the poorest. 'Roseraie de l'Hay' will also stand the salt-laden winds of the seaside.

BOURBONS (Old Garden Roses – Bourbons)

'Mme Isaac Pereire'   Deep cerise pink
Garcon, 1881.

Recurrent roses coming from China, crossed with the
'Autumn Damask', produced the first Western repeat-
flowering family early in the nineteenth century. These
were the Bourbon roses, named after the Ile du Bourbon,
where the first chance cross took place. 'Mme Isaac
Pereire' is one of the very best, provided that there is
room for it, for it will make a 210cm × 150cm (7ft ×
5ft) shrub with enormously strong canes which, because
of their length, will need some support. It can, in fact, be
grown as a short climber. Of all the old roses this is
probably the most fragrant. In the first flush, some of the
huge, sumptuous blooms can be rather misshapen, but
after a brief midsummer pause, those that follow are of
great perfection in every way and come in profusion.
While reasonably healthy, some mildew can be expected
late on, on the fine, dark green leaves. Little black spot.

'Mme Pierre Oger'   Creamy blush pink
Oger, 1978. 'La Reine Victoria' sport.

While most Bourbons have very strong, thick, fairly rigid canes, here they are much more slender, so that a tall stake or a pillar is absolutely essential to keep things under control. With support, 'Mme Pierre Oger' will make a 180cm × 90cm (6ft × 3ft) shrub, so it is one which does not take up a lot of space.

The flowers are some of the most lovely of all, globular, with incurved petals, which are often, and rightly, described as shell-like. They are of a creamy blush, but in the sun this intensifies to a stronger pink, a trait inherited from the China roses in the Bourbon ancestry. They are deliciously scented and appear in clusters, recurrently, tending to be rather smaller in the second flush. The leaves are light green, and while black spot should not be serious, they will need guarding against mildew. 'La Reine Victoria' is similar but a deeper pink.

60

CHINA ROSES (Old Garden Roses – China Roses)

'Old Blush' (also called 'Common Monthly Rose', 'Parson's Pink China')   Light pink with deeper shadings

One of the original roses from China from which all our recurrent varieties are descended, introduced by Parsons in 1796. It makes a spreading, well-branched bush, usually about 120cm × 120cm (4ft × 4ft), on which the crimson-tinted buds open to a silvery-pink with deeper shadings, in loose sprays. If planted against a warm wall, it will make a short climber up to about 240cm (8ft).

China roses are some of the very few that really can be called perpetual. This one will come into bloom early in the summer, and if the weather is not too impossible, there may well still be flowers in midwinter. The whole bush has a daintiness and elegance typical of the group, and the bronze-tinted, rather pointed leaves are exceptionally healthy.

'Hermosa' is another China to try, not quite so vigorous, but with more shapely flowers in a soft lilac-pink.

'Serratipetala'   Crimson, paling towards centre
Vilfroy, 1912.

This is not one of the really old China roses, but the flowers are of the crimson colouring that the Chinas also gave to the West, as well as their recurrent habit. In 'Serratipetala', each bloom pales slightly towards the centre, and in addition they take on a deeper, coppery-crimson hue in hot weather. In the autumn the overall colouring will be lighter, but the really novel feature about the blooms is that the petal edges, as the name of the rose implies, are fringed like a pink. They are most attractive for house decoration and last quite well when cut. As a shrub 'Serratipetala' is quite sturdy but informal in growth, reaching probably 150cm × 150cm (5ft × 5ft), and not making too dense a thicket. The leaves are a very dark green, and could be more plentiful. They are, however, healthy, in common with most Chinas.

Try also 'Mutabilis', in which the flowers change from buff to pink to coppery crimson.

HYBRID PERPETUALS
(Old Garden Roses – Hybrid Perpetuals)

'Baronne Prévost'   Unshaded pink
Desprez, 1842.

One of the earliest Hybrid Perpetuals, this is still one of
the best, the rose pink of the quartered blooms fading
lighter as the flowers age. They are fragrant and repeat
is good. The bush has not the lanky habit of some of this
family and is reasonably compact, growing probably to
about 150cm × 90cm (5ft × 3ft), with a good coverage
of mid-green leaves which will need watching for
mildew in autumn. Where a Hybrid Perpetual does send
up very tall shoots with flowers just at the top, bend
them over in winter rather than prune them, and tie
them to pegs driven into the ground. All the side shoots
will then break and bear flowers.

'Roger Lambelin', a rather less strong-growing variety,
has strongly-scented deep, dusky crimson flowers, the
waved petals edged and streaked with white, a very
pleasing effect.

'Paul Neyron'   Deep rose pink
Levet, 1869. 'Victor Verdier' × 'Anna de Diesbach'.

The Hybrid Perpetuals followed the Bourbons and are
immediate ancesters of the Hybrid Teas. At the time
they were introduced in the nineteenth century they
seemed perpetual in comparison with what had gone
before, but they are not really so. There will be quite a
long gap between the first and second flush of bloom.
'Paul Neyron' is one of the most spectacular, for its huge,
cabbagy blooms are fully 125mm (5in) across, very
double but scarcely scented. As cut flowers they are
sensational.

The bush is one of strong, rigid canes, upright and
probably reaching 150cm × 90cm (5ft × 3ft), with large,
glossy, dark green leaves. Some mildew is likely and
black spot possible.

Another very attractive Hybrid Perpetual, one that
needs good soil to be at its best, is 'Reine des Violettes',
the flowers of which open flat and quartered, a deep
violet-crimson.

HYBRID TEAS (Bush Roses – Large-flowered)

'Adolph Horstmann'   Deep yellow, edged pink
Kordes, 1971. 'Dr A. J. Verhage' × 'Colour Wonder'.

Healthy yellow roses with a good constitution are not
too plentiful. A number suffer from die-back in a severe
winter, and in addition some of the stronger ones, such
as 'Summer Sunshine', tend to be really too tall and long-
stemmed for anything other than a big bed. 'Adolph
Horstmann' is not a short grower, and will reach 90cm
(3ft), but it is quite compact, and the flowers are not
carried too far above the plentiful, large, mid-green,
glossy foliage. They are slightly fragrant, stand rain well,
and are outstanding in the autumn. The flowers are
borne mostly several to a stem, though some will come
singly. Black spot is a possibility. This is a rose to consider
as a possible alternative to 'King's Ransom', which has
held pride of place as a yellow bedding rose for so long,
though its blooms will not so often attain such a fine,
high-centred form. RNRS Trial Ground Certificate,
1972.

'Alec's Red'   Cherry red
Cocker, 1970. 'Fragrant Cloud' × 'Dame de Coeur'.

One of the best bright red Hybrid Teas for bedding, the
glowing colour holding well no matter the weather, and
not dulling as some other red roses do with age. The
blooms can be very large and tend to be more globular
than high-centred, though occasionally they will come
in classic form. The fragrance is quite outstanding, but
resistance to rain a little below average. Nevertheless the
blooms come with great freedom and repeat is quick.
Sometimes they are one to a stem, sometimes in small
clusters, rather tightly grouped.

Growth is strong and upright, with a fair amount of
branching, reaching about 75cm (2ft 6in) in height.
There are plentiful, mid-green, glossy leaves, which on
the whole are very healthy, though there can be some
signs of black spot in autumn. RNRS Gold Medal and
the Edland Medal for fragrance, 1969.

'Alexander' Orange-vermilion
Harkness, 1971. 'Super Star' × ('Ann Elizabeth' ×
'Allgold').

For those who like the striking colour of 'Super Star',
but dislike the mildew to which it is becoming more and
more prone over the years, 'Alexander' is one answer.
The colouring is deeper in the latter variety, and the
blooms do not have so many petals so that, shapely in the
bud, they open more informally and do not hold their
high centres. Not, therefore, a rose for the exhibitor, but
flowers do come very freely, mainly several to a stem,
and over a long period with each flush, with the shortest
pause in between. Fragrance is only slight.

This is a tall, upright rose, which could easily be
classified as a Hybrid Tea-Shrub, for it will generally
reach 120cm (4ft) or so. However, it bushes out well
with plenty of strong canes, which carry dark greem,
semi-glossy leaves. Little sign of disease as a rule, or of
rain damage to the flowers. RNRS Certificate of Merit,
1972, and numerous top awards in other countries as
well.

'Alpine Sunset' Peach pink, flushed yellow
Cant, 1974. 'Dr A. J. Verhage' × 'Grandpa Dickson'.

Though not receiving the highest possible award in its
trial period, this is proving to be, in the garden, one of
the best roses raised in recent years. It seems always to be
in flower, is healthy, a good grower, and the most
attractive blend of colours. The rather globular blooms
are large and come singly and two or three to a stem, the
outer petals opening wide to reveal immaculate high
centres, which hold well if cut for the house, though
perhaps not really long enough for the show bench.
Possibly the overall effect is too rounded for the purist.
'Alpine Sunset' makes a very good bush, vigorous and
with strong canes, branching out well, so that for
bedding it gives a good coverage of the ground. Of
average height, it will reach 75cm (2ft 6in).

The leaves are medium green, glossy, and no more
susceptible to disease than most roses. In other words it
is pretty healthy. Fragrant and a good performer in rainy
weather. RNRS Trial Ground Certificate, 1974.

'Blessings'   Coral pink
Gregory, 1968. 'Queen Elizabeth' × seedling.

It would be very difficult to name a better bedding rose
than this one, and though an offspring of 'Queen
Elizabeth', it will only reach about 75cm (2ft 6in),
making a good, bushy plant. Its strength, however, is in
its freedom of flowering, as it seldom seems to be out of
bloom. It is of the most beautiful, soft coral pink, which
deepens towards the centres of the large, full flowers.
These eventually open wide and are usually borne in
clusters of three or four. Sweetly scented, they stand up
to rainy weather better than most.

The leaves are plentiful, mid-green and semi-glossy.
Roses of the salmon shades are not always noted for their
health, but this one does seem to be an exception – not
completely proof against mildew and black spot, but no
worse than the average. Not a rose for exhibition as the
flower shape does not hold, but ideal as a cut flower for
the house. It gained an RNRS Certificate of Merit in
1968.

'Bonsoir'   Peach pink
Dickson, 1968. Seedling × seedling.

This rose has everything to commend it except that it
does not like rain. In fine weather there is nothing more
lovely than its large, very double and well-shaped
flowers, which are strongly scented. It has won many
show awards, but, for this, protection is needed except in
the sunniest weather. It is an upright, moderately bushy
grower, the flowers generally coming in clusters of three
or four, though well spaced out. Some disbudding will
be needed for them to reach the size of which they are
capable.

Of average vigour, the bush will reach 75cm (2ft 6in),
with plenty of new canes coming from the base. The
leaves are exceptionally large and handsome, leathery,
glossy and very dark green. Some mildew is possible in
late summer, but black spot is not usually a problem. A
rose very much for the exhibitor, and, in the garden, for
a small bed where a wet spell will not matter too much.
RNRS Certificate of Merit, 1966.

'City of Gloucester' — Golden yellow
Sanday, 1970. 'Gavotte' × 'Buccaneer'.

One of the most trouble-free yellow Hybrid Teas there
is, with double blooms of good quality which can reach
considerable size. At their best they are for the show
bench for, though a little on the globular side, they still
have nicely whorled, high, pointed centres when first
opening. However, these are lost after a while, though
this in no way spoils them as a bedding rose. They are
carried singly and several to a stem and are freely
produced, the yellow, with its golden shadings, intensi-
fying considerably in the autumn. The scent is not
strong.

As a plant, 'City of Gloucester' is on the tall side, an
upright grower but a well-branched one which will
reach 90cm (3ft). The matt, mid-green leaves are very
healthy on the whole, and the blooms stand up to rain
remarkably well. So far more popular in the west of
England, where it was raised, it is gradually becoming
more widely known. RNRS Certificate of Merit, 1971.

71

'Doris Tysterman'

Tangerine-orange with deeper petal edges Wisbech Plant Co., 1975. 'Peer Gynt' × seedling.

An upright, vigorous, well-branched variety which will reach 75cm (2ft 6in) and makes an excellent bedding rose, in a colour which has been one of the most popular in recent years, probably because new roses in it have been healthier than in the past. 'Doris Tysterman' may need an eye kept open for mildew, but it is no worse than many another. The flowers are not large, but they are well-formed and there are plenty of them, with a quick repeat and a good performance in the autumn, a time of year when many yellow and orange varieties show to great advantage. The bronze on the petal edges intensifies as the blooms age, making an attractive combination with the bright tangerine-orange of the rest. There is not much scent, but good weather resistance.

The leaves are medium green and glossy, and they cover the plant well. Quite a new rose, showing considerable promise.

'Elizabeth Harkness'

Creamy white, shaded buff and pink Harkness, 1969. 'Red Dandy' × 'Piccadilly'.

Rose breeding is a strange business and full of surprises. Here we have a fine, scarlet-crimson Floribunda crossed with a red and yellow Hybrid Tea, and the result is one of the most lovely Hybrid Teas in creamy white, with both buff and pink shadings. The result must have come from earlier generations, for there is nothing in the immediate parents of 'Red Dandy' or 'Piccadilly' to suggest such colouring in an offspring. The blooms of 'Elizabeth Harkness' are of a classic, high-centred shape which holds well, and they appear very early in the season with satisfactory freedom. Not much trouble from rain, but only a slight fragrance. There will be no out of the ordinary health problems on the upright, bushy plant, which will grow to 75cm (2ft 6in) and is of a compactness that makes it very suitable for bedding. The leaves are semi-glossy and medium green. RNRS Certificate of Merit, 1969.

'Ernest H. Morse'

Turkey-red

Kordes, 1965. Parentage unknown.

The bright Turkey-red blooms of this rose really glow when they first open, but they become a rather duller though still attractive red after a day or so. They can be of classical shape, but there are not too many petals so that they open wide quite quickly, making a very gay show when used for bedding, for which this rose is ideal. There is only the briefest rest period between flushes, and most of the canes bear four or five well-spaced-out flowers at a time. Fragrance is strong and they are quite at home in the rain. The average height is 75cm (2ft 6in) and the strong canes branch quite freely, so that this is a rose to think of when choosing a variety for a standard.

From the health point of view, 'Ernest H. Morse' is well above average, though in a bad season mildew is a possibility. The large, dark green, semi-glossy leaves are bronze-tinted when young. RNRS Gold Medal, 1965.

'Fragrant Cloud'   Dusky geranium-lake
Tantau, 1964. Seedling × 'Prima Ballerina'.

The fragrance of this one, stronger than that of almost any other Hybrid Tea, makes it the perfect answer to those who say that modern roses have no scent. It is of remarkable richness and comes from flowers which open in such profusion and so many to a stem that in its country of origin, Germany, it is classed as Floribunda. The blooms are, however, of full Hybrid Tea size, and can sometimes be very big indeed, high-centred at first but opening to peony form. The colour tends to dull after a day or so, but is still attractive. Rain resistance is above average.

Growth is very strong and well branched, usually reaching about 75cm (2ft 6in) though on soil that suits it especially well it can reach 90cm (3ft). New canes come freely from the base, and the whole plant will be well covered right to the ground with its large, dark green, semi-glossy leaves. Health about average. RNRS Gold Medal, 1963.

'Fred Gibson'   Amber-yellow to apricot
Sanday, 1968. 'Gavotte' × 'Buccaneer'.

Named after a well-known exhibitor, this first made its
name as a show rose, for it has beautifully-shaped, high-
centred flowers, which hold their shape remarkably well
considering that they have comparatively few petals.
However, it soon proved to be equally good in the
garden and particularly so in the autumn. At this time
the flowers, normally a light buff-orange, may be much
paler, with the pink tint which is always present much
more evident. Most blooms come one to a stem early
and then in clusters later. Continuity and rain resistance
is good, but there is very little scent.

A tall, strong and upright grower to about 90cm (3ft),
with long stems which are inclined to be bare of leaves
higher up. There are plenty of leaves lower down,
however, dark green and glossy. There may be some
mildew in later summer. Fairly close planting is advisable
because there is not a great deal of lateral spread. RNRS
Trial Ground Certificate, 1968.

'Gavotte'   Warm pink with silvery reverse
Sanday, 1963. 'Ethel Sanday' × 'Lady Sylvia'.

Wonderful as a cut flower because the blooms hold their
shape so long, this is a rose on which exhibitors always
rely for a good performance. The blooms are very
double and fairly rounded, though with a good, high
centre, but they have little scent. For a rose with so many
petals they stand up to wet weather remarkably well.
'Gavotte' is a very strong grower, though not over tall.
Its plum-red canes branch freely and spread widely,
sometimes bearing their flowers singly, and sometimes
in clusters of three or four. Overall, the height is not
likely to exceed 75cm (2ft 6in).

When young, the leaves are most striking, with deep
red tints, and they mature to a semi-glossy very dark
green, which is equally attractive and unusual. Black
spot is a possibility late in the season. RNRS Certificate
of Merit, 1962.

'Grandpa Dickson'   Soft primrose yellow
Dickson, 1966. ('Perfecta' × 'Governador Braga da
Cruz') × 'Piccadilly'.

The flowers, unlike some other roses which are of top
exhibition quality, shape and size, are equally good for
garden display, as rain does not seem to worry them. It
is not, however, a rose to choose where a bright, glowing
yellow is wanted, but the soft colour has the advantage
that it will blend most happily with others. Sometimes
the petal edges have a faint pink flush. There is little, if
any, scent.

Growth is upright to about 75cm (2ft 6in) without
much lateral spread, so close planting is advised. In most
places it seems vigorous enough, but on sandy soils it is
not at its best and may suffer from some dieback.
Otherwise health is good, with only the possibility of
some black spot in later summer to watch for. The leaves
are on the small side, glossy, light to mid green, and
markedly toothed. RNRS Gold Medal, 1965.

'John Waterer' Deep rose red
McGredy, 1970. 'King of Hearts' × 'Hanne'.

Quite a number of red roses introduced in the 1970s
have received a great deal more publicity than this one
and, in some cases, with much less justification. Its
flowers are of considerable quality, full and high-centred
with large petals, and it is rapidly gaining popularity as
a show rose. It is, however, just as good in the garden, for
it is a free flowerer, the blooms coming sometimes one
to a stem and sometimes in small clusters of three or
four. They stand rain reasonably well and will achieve
considerable size with some disbudding. The scent is,
unfortunately, not strong, a disappointment in a red rose.

New canes come very freely from the base each year,
tough and upright to about 90cm (3ft), clothed with
fine, matt, dark green leaves, which are quite healthy.
RNRS Certificate of Merit, 1969.

'Just Joey'

Coppery-orange, veined red and paling at petal edges
Cant, 1973. 'Fragrant Cloud' × 'Dr. A. J. Verhage'.

In the displays of new seedling varieties not yet in
commerce at the RNRS Summer Show in the season
before 'Just Joey' was put on the market, the public was
asked to vote for them in order of preference. 'Just Joey'
swept the board in a most remarkable way, and it has not
looked back since. Its promise has been more than
fulfilled as a bedding rose, always in flower and carrying
on well into the autumn. The flowers, one to a stem
sometimes, but more often in threes and fours, are
shapely in the bud, though they open fairly quickly to
show their attractively waved petals. Rain resistance is
good. Little scent.

The growth is medium to tall, 75cm (2ft 6in) to 90cm
(3ft), with plenty of strong, flower-bearing laterals. The
leaves are matt and dark green, red-tinted when young.
Health on the whole is good, though black spot is
possible late in the season. RNRS Trial Ground
Certificate, 1971.

'King's Ransom' Rich daffodil yellow
Morey, 1961. 'Golden Masterpiece' × 'Lydia'.

This American rose has for long been considered the best yellow bedding rose. It bears its beautifully-formed, high-centred flowers with great freedom and good continuity, though they are not large for a Hybrid Tea. The yellow fades very little, even in strong sun and there is some scent, though it is not strong. Each flower has up to 40 petals, so they are fully double, and they are very good at keeping going in wet weather. One of its attractions as a bedding plant is the very handsome, glossy, leathery, dark green foliage, which covers the plant well. Vigorous and well-branched, 'King's Ransom' will reach 75cm (2ft 6in), and there are always new canes coming.

Mildew will not usually be a problem, but a watch should be kept for black spot after midsummer. On light soils there can be some die-back in winter. It has never been submitted for trial in Britain.

'Mischief'   Salmon pink
McGredy, 1960, 'Peace' × 'Spartan'.

Few Hybrid Teas flower with the freedom of 'Mischief',
and there will only be the briefest of pauses between
flushes. Unless some disbudding is done the blooms, in
clusters of five or six though well spaced, will not be too
large, though they will all be of fine, classic shape with
high, pointed centres. With disbudding they can grow
to enormous size, and be of exhibition standard. There
is little scent, but they are good in rain.

The bush is very strong and bushy, about 75cm
(2ft 6in) on average, and makes plenty of new growth in
a season. The leaves are medium-sized, light green and
semi-glossy, and cover the plant well. They are, however,
by no means proof against mildew, and in addition this
is a rose which it is best to avoid in districts where rose
rust is likely. Otherwise it makes one of the best of
bedding roses and has long been a favourite. RNRS Gold
Medal, 1961.

'Mister Lincoln' Dark, dusky red
Swim and Weeks, 1964. 'Chrysler Imperial' × 'Charles
Mallerin'.

A great many people, if asked to describe their ideal rose,
would specify one in deep, dusky red, with a strong
fragrance. There have been many such roses, such as the
two parents of this one, but most suffered from mildew,
and the blooms tended to take on an unattractive
purpley-blue tone as they aged. 'Mister Lincoln' is not
completely free from either of these faults, though a
great deal better than most others, but for bedding it
does have a drawback. It is enormously vigorous and
will send up canes to 90–120cm (3–4ft) with clusters of
three to four blooms at the top and not a great deal of
branching lower down. Shapely at first, the flowers open
wide quite quickly to show orange stamens. Strong
sunlight will lighten the colour considerably.

The deep red canes have leathery dark green leaves,
though not too many of them on the long flower stems.
This can, of course, be an advantage when cutting for the
house. 'Mister Lincoln' lasts well in water.

'Mullard Jubilee'   Cerise pink
McGredy, 1970. 'Paddy McGredy' × 'Prima Ballerina'

Both its parents have a liking for mildew, so it is
surprising that it rarely troubles 'Mullard Jubilee',
though black spot may occur after midsummer. This
apart – and there are few other Hybrid Teas which can
claim to be proof against the black spot fungus – it is a
first-rate bedding rose, with very full flowers (about 40
petals) which, though shapely at first, open quite loosely,
which is no worry in the garden. They stand rain well
and are also fragrant. They are mostly carried four or
five to a stem, so that they make a very good display,
with continuity above average.

When picking for the house, in which they will last
well, beware of the very thorny stems. Growth is
vigorous and freely branched to about 75cm (2ft 6in),
and the plentiful leaves are semi-glossy and dark green.
RNRS Gold Medal, 1969.

'My Choice'   Pale pink, reverse pale yellow
Le Grice, 1958. 'Wellworth' × 'Ena Harkness'.

It is difficult to know just why this rose has never been
more widely grown, because it is of the highest quality
for those gardeners who like colours in the more delicate
shades. The soft pink and pale yellow, bicolour blooms
are on the globular side and have the classical high centres
beloved of the exhibitor, but for a rose with so many
petals they open rather quickly, not, however, losing
their charm as a garden variety. Generally they come
several to a stem, and they are extremely fragrant.
Growth is upright, with a reasonable amount of
branching. The height on average is 75cm (2ft 6in),
though in a position which suits it particularly well it
can go a little taller.

The leaves are rather pointed, light green and semi-
glossy. Health is above average, though mildew may
occur late in the year. Flowers come freely, though there
will be a gap of a few weeks between flushes. RNRS
Gold Medal and Clay Vase for fragrance, 1958.

'National Trust'   Red
McGredy, 1970. 'Evelyn Fison' × 'King of Hearts'.

The flowers of this rose have about 60 petals, so they are
extremely double. They are also very shapely, with a
fine, high, whorled centre, but they are never, even with
disbudding, very big, so they do not find favour on the
show bench, even though size is not supposed to count
there against a rose, provided it is true to type. It does,
however, make a fine rose for cutting and will last a long
time in a vase, though it will not scent a room, as
fragrance is singularly lacking. Most of the flowers come
in clusters on each stem with considerable freedom and
with a good continuity, so it is a grand rose for bedding.
Vigorous, upright and well-branched, it will reach on
average 75cm (2ft 6in), with plenty of new growth
coming freely.

The leaves are dark green, matt, and health should be
no particular problem. RNRS Trial Ground Certificate,
1969.

'Pascali'   White, shaded buff
Lens, 1963. 'Queen Elizabeth' × 'White Butterfly'.

There has always been a shortage of good white roses, for the petals of most of them have crumpled in the rain and the bushes been none too healthy. 'Pascali' is, so far, a long way the best, with reasonably rain-proof blooms, and a resistance to disease no worse than other roses, though black spot may appear in late summer. However, the flowers are not in fact pure white, for there is a touch of pale fawn in their centres. For a Hybrid Tea they are on the small side, though always beautifully shaped, and they last well when cut for the house. Generally there are several to a stem.

For bedding, fairly close planting is advisable, for growth is narrow, upright and tall, usually up to about 90cm (3ft), with the flowers at the top. Even hard pruning will not make it branch out very much, and the base of the plant may be a little bare. There will be plenty of light green, glossy leaves higher up. RNRS Certificate of Merit, 1963.

'Peace'

Variable, light to deep yellow, petal edges tinted pink
Meilland, 1942. [('George Dickson' × 'Souv. de Clau-
dius Pernet') × ('Joanna Hill' × 'Charles P. Kilham')]
× 'Margaret McGredy'.

The magnificent blooms of 'Peace' are fully 120–144mm
(5–6in) across, high-centred at first and then cupped,
carried almost always one to a stem, but as growth is
robust and branching there are always plenty of them. It
makes a very big bush which should not be pruned hard
to do well. Moderately cut back it will reach 105cm
(3ft 6in), and lightly treated will top 150cm (5ft),
making it a good hedging rose or useful as a specimen.
For bedding, the planting distance should be 90cm (3ft).

In 1976 an international vote declared 'Peace' the
world's favourite rose, but this was not simply because
of its fine flowers. It was also because it has large, dark
green, glossy leaves on which it is very rare to see any
sign of disease. A lack of scent is its only real failing, and
it is also one of the last roses to come into bloom. But
then, what a show! RNRS Gold Medal, 1947.

'Peer Gynt'   Canary yellow, flushed pink
Kordes, 1968. 'Colour Wonder' × 'Golden Giant'.

'Golden Giant' used to wave its blooms about on the end
of 150cm (5ft) stems, but 'Colour Wonder' is a short,
stubby grower, and luckily 'Peer Gynt' has taken after
the second parent. It is, however, much more bushy, and
flowers and new canes come much more freely, reaching
a maximum of 75cm (2ft 6in). The blooms are rather
globular in shape and many of them will open cupped,
so it is a rose to make the garden gay rather than one for
the show bench. The edges of the petals are often tinged
with pink, and this colour intensifies as the flowers age.
There is slight fragrance only. Continuity is extremely
good, and the blooms are outstanding in the autumn,
when the overall colour may be deeper. The leaves are
large, semi-glossy, and a rather light green. Black spot is
no worse than average, but guard this rose against
mildew. RNRS Certificate of Merit, 1967.

89

'Piccadilly'   Scarlet with yellow reverse
McGredy, 1959. 'McGredy's Yellow' × 'Karl Herbst'.

This rose has been around for quite a long time, during which many other red and yellow bicolours have come and gone. There has been nothing to rival it, even though, as the flowers age the red suffuses the yellow and the striking contrast of the two colours is lost. The blooms, shapely at first, open wide later and are of medium size. There is no noticeable scent, but outstanding performance in the rain and in the autumn to compensate. Freedom of flowering is exceptionally good right through the summer.

'Piccadilly' makes a strong, well-branched bush, always with plenty of new growth. When young, the leaves are deep red, which changes as they age to a dark, glossy green with bronze tints, a combination which sets off the flowers particularly well. Health is generally above average with mildew seldom troublesome, but there can be a little black spot in autumn. RNRS Certificate of Merit, 1969. It should have been a Gold Medal.

'Pink Favourite'   Deep rose pink
Von Abrams, 1956. 'Juno' × ('Georg Arends' × 'New
Dawn').

A prolific bloomer, the flowers of which come in
closely-packed clusters at the top of very strong canes, so
that some disbudding really has to be done if they are not
to cramp each other on opening. If only one per stem is
left, they will reach an enormous size, and because of
their symmetrical and high-centred form they have
frequently featured as Best Bloom of the Show. At times,
however, they can be rather coarse and the pink lacks
delicacy. The lesser-known sport of 'Pink Favourite',
'Honey Favourite' is a much more refined rose, and the
outstanding feature of both is that they are practically
immune to both mildew and black spot. Probably this
is the reason that 'Pink Favourite' has lasted at the top of
the popularity charts as long as it has.

The strong, upright growth will reach 90cm (3ft) and
the leaves are large, dark green and glossy, fairly glowing
with robust health.

'Precious Platinum'   Cardinal red
Dickson, 1974. 'Red Planet' × 'Franklin Engelmann'.

One of a series of fine red Hybrid Teas from this Irish
raiser, which have included 'Red Devil' and Gold Medal
winner 'Red Planet'. 'Precious Platinum' did not get an
award in the United Kingdom though it did get a
Certificate of Merit in New Zealand. It is proving to be
a more popular bedding rose than 'Red Planet', despite
the fact that it must be watched for mildew. The bright
colour of the blooms really glows, and there is a sweet
scent to go with it. The well-shaped blooms can be of
exhibition quality, but after a shapely bud stage they can
open a little loose, and generally speaking quite a lot of
disbudding would be needed to bring them above
medium size. Otherwise they come in clusters of three
or four with great freedom. 75cm (2ft 6in) will be the
average height, vigorous and nicely branched, with
medium green, semi-glossy leaves which cover the plant
well.

'Red Devil'   Scarlet with lighter reverse
Dickson, 1967. 'Silver Lining' × 'Prima Ballerina'.

Certainly no rose in recent years has carried off more top awards on the show bench than 'Red Devil'. It is rare for it to produce a bloom that is not of perfect shape and the highest quality, and when cut the flowers seem to last for ever. Continuity is good for a rose with such large blooms, which come one to a stem early in the year and in clusters of two or three later. They are richly fragrant, but they are not very happy in the rain, which is a drawback for bedding. In a good summer this rose can, however, be magnificent, for it is a strong, outstandingly healthy grower, with very robust canes reaching 90cm (3ft) in height. Though plenty of new growth comes from ground level, it does not branch out over-much, and so should not be too widely spaced when planting.

An outstanding feature, quite apart from the flowers, is the very large, deep green, semi-glossy foliage. RNRS Certificate of Merit, 1967.

'Rose Gaujard'

White, flushed carmine, with silvery reverse
Gaujard, 1958. 'Peace' × 'Opera'.

This is often described as a beginners' rose, by which is meant that it is very tough and vigorous and will grow practically anywhere. It will make a large, well-branched bush probably 90cm (3ft) in height, and to allow for its size bushes should be planted about 75cm (2ft 6in) apart. The large, dark green, glossy foliage is above average in its resistance to disease, and the flowers are almost impervious to rain. Many of them come one to a stem, particularly in the first flush, and they can reach an enormous size. They are invariably of immaculate, high-centred form in the bud, but quite a high proportion of them are likely to have split centres when they open more fully. This matters on the show bench, but is not of too much importance in the garden. The important thing is that there will always be plenty of them, for continuity is very good and the overall effect in a bed good. RNRS Gold Medal, 1958.

'Silver Jubilee' Peach blends
Cocker, 1978. [('Parkdirektor Riggers' × 'Piccadilly')
× ('Highlight' × 'Colour Wonder')] × 'Mischief'.

Named by permission of Her Majesty Queen Elizabeth
II in celebration of her Jubilee, no rose could be more
fitting of the honour. Apart from the beautiful blend of
colours in its blooms, which hold their high-centred
shape remarkably well considering that there are not a
great many petals, the flowers come with tremendous
freedom and the petals fall cleanly when they are over.
The colour tends to intensify in hot sunshine, rather than
fade as so many roses do. There is some scent, though not
outstanding, and rain resistance is above average. For
really large blooms, early disbudding is advised, but in
the garden none at all should be needed.

Of ideal bedding height, 75cm (2ft 6in), with plenty
of strong, well-branched canes, covered right down to
the ground with handsome, glossy, medium green leaves
which do not seem to know the meaning of the word
disease. RNRS Gold Medal, 1977.

'Silver Lining'   Silvery pink, silver reverse
Dickson, 1958. 'Karl Herbst' × 'Eden Rose' seedling.

A rose in the most delicate colours and of great refinement, its great fragrance adds to its other attractions. The blooms are always beautifully formed with tightly scrolled, high centres, which hold well so that it is a rose for the show bench. However, it stands up to rain and so is equally suitable for the garden.

The majority of flowers come one to a stem and they can reach a considerable size, 100–120mm (4–5in) across at their best. Growth is vigorous and well branched up to about 75cm (2ft 6in), with plenty of new canes coming from the base. The leaves are on the small side, dark green and glossy, and cover the plant well. They will, however, need watching for black spot after midsummer, though mildew is unlikely to be a serious problem. A good rose for bedding and of a colour which makes it useful for separating other varieties which might clash if put next to each other. RNRS Gold Medal, 1958 and Clay Vase for fragrance, 1957.

'Stella'   Cream and pink blends
Tantau, 1959. 'Horstmann's Jubiläumrose' × 'Peace'.

Though classed as a Hybrid Tea in the United Kingdom,
elsewhere it is sometimes considered a Grandiflora, that
is, a tall-growing Floribunda with large flowers for the
type. Certainly it will go up to 90cm (3ft) or slightly
more, with plenty of strong canes but not a great deal of
branching. It does, too, bear a great many of its flowers
at the top in small clusters, but not always so. However,
to get real size, blooms 100–120mm (4–5in) across, some
disbudding is likely to be needed. If this is done, real
show roses will be produced, high-centred and immaculate which, despite the fact that they are very full, are
quite unaffected by rain. It is one of the best of roses in
this respect, and so is a first-rate garden variety, for the
back of the border, perhaps, rather than for a small bed.

The leaves are very glossy, large and leathery, not
proof against black spot, or against rust in rust-prone
areas. RNRS Gold Medal, 1960.

'Summer Holiday'   Orange-vermilion, paler reverse
Gregory, 1969. 'Super Star' × unknown.

It is a pity that the two best-known roses in orange-
vermilion colouring, 'Super Star' and 'Duke of Windsor'
should be so poor from the health point of view, but
there are alternatives which are a great deal better, even
if the tones are rather deeper in each case. 'Alexander', a
tall one, is described on p. 67, but for a bedding rose of
average height 'Summer Holiday' fills the gap admirably.
The blooms are very full, fragrant, and come sometimes
singly and sometimes in small clusters. They are very
free and quick to repeat. They do not mind rain, though
sometimes they can become rather heavy for the flower
stalks when wet. 75–90cm (2ft 6in–3ft) will be reached
by the vigorous, spreading bush. It has plenty of semi-
glossy leaves, which have a red tinge to them. Health is
a bit above average. RNRS Trial Ground Certificate,
1968.

'Tenerife'   Orange/coral/salmon with peach reverse
Bracegirdle, 1972. 'Fragrant Cloud' × 'Piccadilly'.

One of the few roses raised by an amateur to meet with
considerable commercial success, and well deserving it.
The colouring of coral and apricot-orange varies
considerably with the weather conditions, and the
reverse of the petals can be either apricot or pale yellow,
but all the combinations are equally attractive. A little
on the globular side, the blooms come mainly one to a
stem, do not mind the rain, are very fragrant, and appear
freely until well into the autumn. Growth is vigorous
and upright to average bedding rose height with strong
canes and reasonable branching. The leaves are glossy,
medium green, large and tinted bronze when young.
They may need protection from black spot. The chances
of an amateur breeding a new variety which leading
growers want on their list are very small. Few achieve
the necessary individuality and quality, but 'Tenerife'
also gained a RNRS Trial Ground Certificate in 1972.

'Troika' Apricot to orange, edged and veined scarlet
Poulsen, 1972. Parentage unknown.

There have been many roses in various shades of orange,
but few which have not been subject to die-back and all
the other rose ills. 'Troika' has not been with us very
long, but so far it shows promise of being what we have
been looking for in this colour. Black spot is a possibility
in late summer, but otherwise it is healthy. The flowers
are large, full and very well formed. Wet weather does
not seem to worry them, and they are strongly scented
as well. In general they come one to a stem early on, and
in clusters of three or four later on. Continuity is first
rate.

'Troika' will reach 75cm (2ft 6in) and sometimes
rather more. Growth is strong and moderately bushy,
with large, glossy, mid-green leaves, which have bronze
tints when they are young. All in all, a first-rate rose for
both the garden and for the show bench, which cannot
be said of many others. RNRS Certificate of Merit, 1973.

'Typhoon'   Coppery-orange/salmon
Kordes, 1972. 'Colour Wonder' × 'Dr A. J. Verghage'.

Like 'Tenerife', this is a rose in which the colour can vary
considerably, though this time with the time of year
rather than the weather. In the autumn, the coppery-
orange turns almost to flame, though the bases of the
petals retain their yellow tones. Mostly coming one to a
stem, the blooms are on the globular side, some opening
cupped. Recurrence is good, as is the autumn performance, so that there are few days during the season when
no blooms are showing. A good, upright and reasonably
bushy bedding rose, it will reach about 75cm (2ft 6in),
very well covered with its semi-glossy, mid-green leaves,
which have strong red tints when they first come in late
spring. Reports on its health have been good from all
parts of the country, but the same cannot be said for its
scent, which is only slight. Planted in the mass this really
makes a most striking contribution to any garden. RNRS
Certificate of Merit, 1972.

'Wendy Cussons'　　　　　　　　　　Deep cerise pink
Gregory, 1959. 'Independence' × 'Eden Rose'.

A bedding rose with every desirable quality save one. It is very robust and branches out well, its red canes carrying an apparently inexhaustible number of flowers of immaculate shape, ranging from large to medium in size and very sweetly scented. They are, however, of a very strong cerise pink, which is not to everyone's taste, and they need careful placing in relation to other roses. With some reds, especially, they will clash horribly. Rain resistance is good and the bush will grow to 75cm (2ft 6in), with quite a wide sideways spread. Every side shoot bears at least one flower, with a quick repeat. The dark green, semi-glossy leaves are sometimes tinted and edged red, and though health generally is good, they are not quite proof against mildew.

Though primarily an almost ideal bedding rose, because of its widely branching habit 'Wendy Cussons' makes a very good standard. RNRS Gold Medal, 1959.

'Yellow Pages'   Bright yellow
McGredy, 1972. 'Arthur Bell' × 'Peer Gynt'.

The blooms of this rose have about 40 petals and so they
are fully double, which generally means that the shape
holds well. Here the classic form is present in the early
stages, but then the flowers open out more loosely,
though they are still equally attractive and make 'Yellow
Pages' a wonderful bedding rose, almost always in
flower. Some blooms come singly and some in small
clusters, often with a pink flush, and repeating quickly.
Only a slight fragrance, but very good weather resistance,
so that a bed of it will never become unsightly with
sodden blooms.

Growth is vigorous and bushy, with plenty of new
canes, and it will make a compact plant about 75cm
(2ft 6in) high. Semi-glossy, light green rather small
leaves complete the picture, and it seems a pity that such
an attractive rose was not given a more attractive name.
RNRS Trial Ground Certificate, 1971.

103

CLIMBERS
(Climbing Roses – Recurrent and Non-recurrent)

'Bantry Bay'   Pink
McGredy, 1967. 'New Dawn' × 'Korona'.

Shapely in the bud, the semi-double flowers open wide
to some 70mm (3in) across, and the flowers are well
spaced in the trusses. They are very free and recurrent,
but almost completely lacking in scent. The semi-glossy,
medium green foliage is generally very healthy, though
reports of black spot have come from certain areas.
Growth is vigorous, but as it will not usually exceed
240–270cm (8–9ft) 'Bantry Bay' makes a good pillar
rose or one for a low wall. RNRS Certificate of Merit,
1967.

'Swan Lake' of 1968 is another fine, recurrent
McGredy rose, with very double, high-centred flowers
in white with a pink tinge in the centre, carried mainly
in small clusters. Probably the best white climber, despite
the fact that the petals do not drop cleanly when the
flower fades. It is vigorous to about 240cm (8ft), and
may need some protection from black spot.

'Cécile Brunner'   Pale pink
Ducher, 1880. A climbing sport of the bush form.

'Cécile Brunner' in its original form is a very dainty, 90cm × 60cm (3ft × 2ft) shrub, a cross between a Tea rose and a Polyantha and in all ways, except habit of growth, identical to the climber. Surprisingly the climbing sport is enormously vigorous and will certainly reach 6m (20ft), suitable for walls, pergolas and above all for climbing into trees. It was first discovered in 1904.

Known also as The Sweetheart Rose because of its tiny but perfectly formed buds, it will have a tremendous crop first time round and a less exuberant showing later on. When fully open, the blooms are loose and informal, with little if any scent. The leaves are an attractive feature, narrow and pointed, with bronze tints in the dark green and never a trace of disease. When young, the canes are a purplish-red, and there are not too many thorns. First flowering will be in early summer.

'Compassion'   Salmon-orange with lighter reverse
Harkness, 1973. 'White Cockade' × 'Prima Ballerina'.

The colouring of 'Compassion' is unusual among
climbing roses, so this is a welcome addition to the
range, particularly as it is a profuse bloomer and has a
good repeat in late summer. Small to medium trusses are
the norm. The strong, upright growth will go up to
about 240cm (8ft), so it makes an ideal pillar rose, or it
can be useful for the walls of a single storey house. The
glossy, dark green leaves are healthy as a rule. RNRS
Henry Edland Medal for fragrance was awarded in 1973.

Really the only other climber of roughly similar
colouring is 'Schoolgirl', with full, 96mm (4in), burnt-
orange flowers which fade paler and may have a touch
of salmon at times. Recurrence is good, but rain can
damage the blooms. Vigorous to 240–300cm (8–10ft).

'Danse du Feu' Orange-scarlet
Mallerin, 1954. 'Paul's Scarlet Climber' × *R. multiflora*
seedling.

A rose with a tremendous reputation and which can be
found in every nursery list. It was one of the first really
popular modern repeat-flowering varieties, and its
orange-scarlet blooms do put on a tremendous display
with a good repeat. Unfortunately, they rather quickly
lose their brilliance, ageing to a colour which clashes
horribly with newly-opened flowers, and the petals do
not drop cleanly. It will need early training to keep it
flowering low down, but is a vigorous grower to about
300cm (10ft), with attractive, glossy dark green leaves,
bronze-tinted when young. Generally it is healthy,
though mildew can be troublesome on dry soils. A rose
for a spectacular show on a wall or pillar, but for a really
good, if slightly darker, red climber perhaps 'Parkdirektor Riggers' is a better bet, though 'Danse du Feu' was a
RNRS Certificate of Merit rose in 1954.

'Gloire de Dijon'

Buff yellow, with pink and orange tints Jacotot, 1853. Possibly an unknown Tea rose × 'Souvenir de la Malmaison', or possibly a Tea rose × a Noisette climber.

An historic climber, and still one of the earliest into bloom in late spring and seldom without flowers later. It was one of the first hybrids with yellow-toned Tea-style flowers ever raised, though the yellow is mingled with pink and orange. The blooms are large and very double, scented, and grow in small clusters, and though not of particularly good form, make a fine display in the mass. Some blooms are quartered in the old style. On a wall it will reach 4.5m (15ft) and is best with no pruning, though if it gets bare at the base, one or two main canes can be cut back to 180–240cm (6–8ft) to encourage new growth. The leaves are mid-green and can be attacked by mildew.

Certain breeding stock of this rose has deteriorated over the years, so it is important to order from a reliable nursery.

'Golden Showers'   Bright yellow
Lammerts, 1956. 'Charlotte Armstrong' × 'Capt. Thomas'.

Long, pointed buds open quite quickly for there are not a great many petals, which also makes the flower form loose and informal, though attractively waved. The bright, golden yellow fades a little with age, but rain does not trouble the blooms at all. Its flowering period is from early summer to the end of autumn, and there will seldom be a time when no flowers are showing at all during these months. Hips do, however, form readily, and these should be snipped off after the first flush if the full potential is to be achieved. This is not too difficult to do, as normally 'Golden Showers' will not go over 210–240cm (7–8ft), and the smooth, reddish canes have very few thorns. An upright grower, it does not spread out very much unless helped by training, but as it bears plenty of flowers even without this it is a useful rose for a narrow space, perhaps between two tall windows.

'Handel'   Creamy white, edged carmine
McGredy, 1965. 'Columbine' × 'Hamburg'.

One of the most successful repeat-flowering climbers to
have been introduced in recent years. The blooms, while
moderately full, are not really double, and open wide
and slightly cupped. The rosy pink of the petal edges
suffuses the whole flower as it ages, still looking attractive
if not quite so unusual. Fragrance is only very slight, but
resistance to rain very good. Probably 'Handel' will go
up to 4.5 m (15 ft) or so, with plenty of strong laterals and
new growth coming from the base. The leaves are semi-
glossy, dark green and have bronze tints. They will need
watching for black spot.

A good rose for a wall, pillar or fence and quite easy
to train if this is carried out from the beginning before
the sturdy canes become too rigid. Branching freely, it
carries plenty of bloom at all levels. RNRS Trial Ground
Certificate, 1965.

'Pink Perpêtue'   Pink
Gregory, 1965. 'Danse du Feu' × 'New Dawn'.

The clear pink of the full, rather globular blooms deepens to carmine pink on the reverse of the petals, and they are carried with great profusion in medium-sized clusters, being particularly good in the autumn. Its raiser recommends a light cutting-back of the laterals after the first flush to encourage new flowering shoots for later on. There is very little, if any, fragrance, though it is always difficult to be dogmatic about this as scent can vary with the time of day and the humidity of the air – and with an individual's sense of smell.

Vigour seems to vary somewhat, but at all times it should be tall enough for a pillar. Firm training is needed to encourage it to branch out well, but if this is done 'Pink Perpêtue' is one of the most rewarding climbers in its colour range. With some support, it can be grown as a small shrub. RNRS Certificate of Merit, 1964.

'Albertine' Coppery-pink
Barbier, 1921. *R. luciae* × 'Mrs A. R. Waddell'.

Certainly one of the loveliest ramblers ever raised, and belonging to the comparatively small group that flower early. The sheer mass of bloom, coming from coppery-pink buds is breathtaking, and the scent will float in the air for yards around. It sends up long and enormously strong and thorny canes with great freedom, and firm training is needed to keep it within bounds, together with regular cutting out of the old wood which has flowered, once the bloom has gone. Which brings me to 'Albertine's' one weakness; it does not shed its old petals any too well, and if rain comes when they are dying they just become sodden and do not drop. Though only blooming once, it does carry on for a number of weeks, and is a first-rate rose for an arch or pergola or for covering a garden shed, but not for walls, because mildew can be a problem with it. Dark green leaves.

'American Pillar' — Strong pink with white eye
Dr W. Van Fleet, 1902. (*R. wichuraiana* × *R. setigera*) × a red Hybrid Perpetual.

Because at one time it was planted everywhere, gardeners became a little tired of this rose and tended to decry its merits. Some people, too, did not admire its bright rose pink, though the white eye of each flower makes it very striking. For sheer mass of bloom there is scarcely anything to touch it, the single flowers coming in huge trusses on stiff stems which branch out from the main canes. It is a rampant grower for an arch or pergola, with glossy, dark green leaves, which will need watching for mildew. Summer flowering only. It will make a large, informal shrub as well as climb, and as in this form it looks rather different, with its long canes arching outwards instead of mounting upwards, it is well worth giving it a second chance in the modern garden using it in this way. Very little fragrance unfortunately.

113

'Seagull'   White
Pritchard, 1907.

This is one of a large group of white ramblers which carry huge heads of comparatively small flowers, in most cases very sweetly scented, which if grown up a tree, will hang down from its branches like a creamy waterfall throughout the latter half of the summer. The flowers of 'Seagull' are larger than some of the others, and are lit up by bright yellow stamens. It will go up to about 6m (20ft), as will 'Thalia', 'Rambling Rector' and 'The Garland'. Others are even taller, and 'Silver Moon' will reach 12m (40ft). One of these roses alone will, in time, cover a substantial pergola, but the pergola must be a strong one if it is not to collapse under the weight of the freely-branching canes. 'Seagull' is one of the scented ones, with good foliage, which is quite healthy, but do not be tempted into buying it unless you really do have room to let it ramble freely.

114

POLYANTHAS (Bush Roses – Polyanthas)

'The Fairy'   Soft pink
Bentall, 1932. Classed as a Polyantha, though actually a
sport from the rambler 'Lady Godiva'.

Polyanthas were enormously popular at one time, before
they were crossed with Hybrid Teas and became
Floribundas with much larger flowers and taller growth.
There are only a very few left on the market now, and of
these, 'The Fairy' is certainly the best. The blooms are
globular and carried in very large heads on stiff stems,
forming a bushy plant not more than 60cm (2ft) tall.
There is plenty of very glossy, light green foliage, which
may need watching for black spot, but mildew, the curse
of so many Polyanthas, is rare. No discernible scent.

This is an ideal rose for growing on a patio or
anywhere else where something small and dainty is
needed. It also, as in the picture, makes a good low hedge
to surround a pool or to divide one part of a garden from
another. Enthusiastically recurrent.

FLORIBUNDAS (Bush Roses – Cluster-flowered)

'Allgold'   Golden yellow
Le Grice, 1956. 'Goldilocks' × 'Ellinor Le Grice'.

The bright, golden yellow of 'Allgold' does not fade to cream in strong sun as with so many other yellow roses, and this is its greatest attraction. The flowers come in small trusses, sometimes of as few as two to three blooms, though more usually with six or seven. Fragrance is very slight, and they make a loose, informal flower, which rain hardly affects at all.

A naturally short grower to not much over 60cm (2ft), branching is quite prolific but not always very even. Close planting will make this rather less obvious, and quite hard pruning will also help to keep it more uniform in its behaviour. The rather small, light green, very glossy leaves could be more plentiful, but they are practically disease free. This, and the permanence of its colour, make up for some faults that are really not too serious. RNRS Gold Medal, 1956.

'Anne Cocker'   Light vermilion
Cocker, 1971. 'Highlight' × 'Colour Wonder'.

One of the outstanding qualities of this rose is the length
of time it will last if cut for the house. Few varieties will
last for a week or ten days without looking tired, but this
one will, possibly because of its full, rounded blooms,
packed with short petals. They are equally good in the
garden, and come with great freedom on good-sized
trusses. A large number of petals often means trouble in
the rain, when they tend to stick together so that the
blooms 'ball', but not here. There is little, if any, scent.

The strong, vigorous stems, which branch well, may
reach 90cm (3ft), and new growth forms rapidly to
ensure good continuity. The leaves are a darkish green
with red tints, especially when young, and are semi-
glossy. Health is good on the whole, but mildew should
be watched for after midsummer. RNRS Certificate of
Merit, 1969.

'Anne Harkness'   Deep apricot-orange
Harkness, 1980. Floribunda-Hybrid Tea. 'Bobby Daz-
zler' × [('Manx Queen' × 'Prima Ballerina') × ('Chanelle' × 'Piccadilly')].

A really beautiful rose with large, double flowers, well-
spaced in the truss and having attractively waved petals.
It has all the qualities needed for bedding and for a
hedging rose, as it is a tall grower up to about 105cm (3ft
6in), an upright, bushy plant with plenty of well-
branched main canes. It is very free-flowering once it
gets under way, but it is rather a late starter, waiting
until well into high summer, which some people may
consider a disadvantage. However, this does mean that
it is likely to be in full bloom while others are resting, a
welcome and cheerful splash of warm colour that goes
on and on. There is not much scent, but Harkness roses
have a great reputation for good health, to which
particular attention is paid in their breeding lines. Its
semi-glossy, medium green leaves are very resistant to
disease. RNRS Trial Ground Certificate, 1978.

'Arthur Bell'   Golden yellow, fading creamy yellow
McGredy, 1965. 'Cläre Grammerstorf' × 'Piccadilly'.

The large flowers with big petals are shapely at first and
open wide to a deep golden yellow, which quite soon
fades to a creamy yellow that is just as attractive but
different. Continuity is good, with trusses, though only
of medium size, which seem large because of the size of
the sweetly-scented flowers. 'Arthur Bell' is a tall grower
and will usually reach 90cm (3ft), with strong new canes
coming exceptionally freely from the base and branching
out well, so that despite its height it never looks leggy.
Particularly good and plentiful large, semi-glossy leaves,
leathery in texture, cover the plant right down to the
ground, so that when it is used for bedding, weeds have
very little chance of flourishing anywhere near it – there
is just no light left for them.

Health is above average, though there is no absolute
guarantee against either mildew or black spot. RNRS
Certificate of Merit, 1964.

'City of Belfast' Velvety scarlet
McGredy, 1968. 'Evelyn Fison' × ('Korona' × 'Circus').

If you are looking for a fine, velvety-scarlet bedding rose which does not grow too tall and which will be almost constantly in flower, you cannot really do better than this one. It is not enormously vigorous, but makes a very compact and freely branching plant which will reach about 60cm (2ft). It will be very well covered with glossy, mid-green leaves of above average health and which are attractively red-tinted when young.

For a Floribunda, the flowers are large, some being up to 72mm (3in) across, but the trusses are not overly big, even though the number of them and the freedom and frequency with which they come more than makes up for this. Rain is no problem and leaves the blooms unmarked. In addition to normal bedding in the garden, this is a rose to consider for quite a small patio. The colour would brighten it, without being too dazzling in a small space. RNRS Gold Medal, 1967.

'City of Leeds'   Rich salmon pink
McGredy, 1966. 'Evelyn Fison' × ('Spartan' × 'Red
Favourite').

The flowers, shapely in the bud stage, open wide on
medium-sized, well-spaced trusses, which are carried on
very strong, well-branched canes. Growth is bushy, so
that it makes a very good bedding rose, reaching about
75cm (2ft 6in) on average. The most attractive colour is
only spoiled by a tendency of the blooms to spot after
heavy and prolonged rain. Continuity is, however,
extremely good, so that there are almost always fresh
flowers waiting to take the place of the old when the sun
shines again. There are plenty of leaves to cover the plant
well at all levels, even if individually they are rather on
the small side. Vigilance is needed against mildew late in
the season, but black spot is not usually troublesome.

It is a pity that such a beautiful rose has not much
scent, but despite this it is very worthwhile where
strident colours would be out of place. RNRS Gold
Medal, 1965.

'Courvoisier'　　　　　　　　　　　　　　　Ochre yellow
McGredy, 1970. Floribunda-Hybrid Tea. 'Elizabeth of
Glamis' × 'Casanova'.

Its classification indicates that this is not a normal, small-
flowered Floribunda, but even within the category in
which it falls the flowers are very big and double, having
over 50 petals. Some come singly and some in clusters,
so that all together it would be difficult to argue with
somebody who considered it a full Hybrid Tea. As has
been shown the differences between the two groups are
becoming less and less distinct, and this is not the only
case where a decision could go either way.

Growth is moderately vigorous and upright, and
there is glossy, leathery, mid-green foliage, which may
need watching for black spot. A reasonable degree of
branching makes for quite a bushy plant of average
height for bedding, which means about 75cm (2ft 6in).
The blooms are fragrant. RNRS Trial Ground Certificate, 1969.

'Coventry Cathedral'　　　　　　　　Orange-vermilion
McGredy, 1972. Floribunda-Hybrid Tea. ('Little Darling' × 'Goldilocks') × 'Irish Mist'.

A rose which is proving a better performer in gardens
now that it is established than seemed likely when it was
first introduced, and it makes a very gay bed when
planted in the mass, helped by the fact that it is extremely
free-flowering and has a quick repeat. The official
description of the colour is light vermilion, but really
there is more orange in it than that would imply. The
reverse of the moderately full flowers, which open wide,
is paler, and they come on large and well-spaced trusses.
Little scent and some spotting after heavy rain are their
only drawbacks. The plant will reach 75cm (2ft 6in) to
90cm (3ft), strong-growing and upright, with plenty of
canes coming from the crown and branching out well.
The green of the leaves is on the light side, and they are
semi-glossy. On light soils a certain amount of die-back
has been experienced, but not too serious. Otherwise
health seems about average. RNRS Trial Ground
Certificate, 1971.

'Dame of Sark'   Gold, flushed scarlet
Harkness, 1976. ('Pink Parfait' × 'Masquerade') ×
'Tabler's Choice'.

This is a tall one which will make a very good hedge of
the sort of stature needed for lining a drive or for either
side of a garden path. It can, of course, also be used for
bedding and looks wonderful in the mass, though it
would be most suitable for a bed of some size. The taller
roses do rather tend to overwhelm a small one.

'Dame of Sark' will reach 90cm (3ft), very vigorous
and upright, with always plenty of new growth coming,
combined with reasonable branching. Basically an
orange rose, there is also a good deal of yellow in the
make-up, which gives it an extra brightness. The trusses
are of medium size and there is a quick repeat. Not,
however, very much scent in the full, double blooms,
but they do stand up to rough weather well. RNRS Trial
Ground Certificate, 1976.

'Dearest'   Soft pink

Dickson, 1960. A 'Spartan' seedling.

A favourite with everybody since its introduction, not
only for its beautiful soft colouring, but because it has a
fine perfume with a hint of cloves. The blooms are large
and full of petals, opening flat to show creamy-yellow
stamens, and are carried on big flat trusses with
tremendous freedom. Apart from a tendency to fade a
little after some days, their one real failing is a dislike of
rain, though they do not seem to mind a damp, misty
day such as is frequently encountered in autumn, when
the rose flowers very well without any signs of distress.
It is long-lasting as a cut flower.

Strong and bushy, it will reach an average height of
75cm (2ft 6in), and though there is a short pause between
flushes, continuity is good. New growth from the base
forms rapidly. The dark green, glossy leaves need
watching for black spot. RNRS Gold Medal, 1961.

125

'Elizabeth of Glamis'   Orange, salmon-pink
McGredy, 1964. 'Spartan' × 'Highlight'.

The soft, salmon-pink, deepening in the heart of the flower, makes this one of the most beautiful of roses, and it is richly scented, too. The blooms open wide to 60–70mm (2½–3in) across, coming from shapely, high-centred buds, repeating quickly and seeming to revel especially in hot, dry weather. The trusses can be very large, and are always well spaced out.

The tall, upright plant will probably reach 90cm (3ft), but unfortunately seems only to be at its best on light soils. In cold areas with heavy soils it has proved unreliable. It is reputed not to transplant well, but this may depend on where it is transplanted to, and it is of such quality that these doubts about its fitness should deter nobody, wherever they live. Because of the above, it is difficult to generalise about health, but there can be some mildew anywhere. RNRS Gold Medal and Clay Vase for fragrance, 1963.

'English Holiday'   Yellow, flushed salmon pink
Harkness, 1977. 'Bobby Dazzler' × 'Goldbonnet'.

The frilly petals of this rose are perhaps not quite double
enough to make true pompons, but they are not far from
it. The yellow, suffused and edged with salmon pink is
a very pleasing combination and reminiscent of the
Floribunda 'Circus' which was popular for many years.
However, the flowers have a fragrance which the older
rose lacked. Good in the rain, they are carried in
medium-sized trusses, which come freely and bloom on
well into the autumn, when the colour may be a little
deeper. Growth is very vigorous with plenty of canes
coming from the crown, and as it will reach 90cm (3ft)
its use for hedging as well as bedding is suggested. Tall
as it is, not all the growing energy goes upwards, so that
it is bushy enough to make a good screen, filled in with
plentiful, glossy, medium green leaves. Very little trouble
will be experienced with the common rose diseases.
RNRS Trial Ground Certificate, 1976.

'English Miss' Silvery pink, edged deeper
Cant, 1977. 'Dearest' × 'Sweet Repose'.

Floribundas of the delicate pink and charm of 'English
Miss' are rare indeed, and so it is especially welcome on
that account alone. One really has to go back to 1960 to
'Dearest' (one of its parents) to find another equally good,
though there are many differences in the flower form.
The buds of 'English Miss' are very shapely, resembling
camellias when the petals expand further. They have a
sweet scent and are borne on both large and medium-
sized trusses with great freedom and a quick repeat. A
bowl cut for the house just as the blooms are opening
will last for several days without losing its freshness.

Growth is very strong and it will make a bushy plant,
as there are plenty of side shoots from the main canes.
75cm (2ft 6in) is the average height, so for bedding this
is one to pick, especially if you need something restful.
Healthy, glossy leaves, too. RNRS Trial Ground
Certificate, 1977.

'Escapade'   Lilac-rose with light eye
Harkness, 1967. 'Pink Parfait' × 'Baby Faurax'.

'Escapade's' unique colour (for a Floribunda) came from
'Baby Faurax', a Polyantha dating back to 1924, though
it must be said that there is some fade in strong sunshine.
However, this does not lessen the flower's attractiveness,
and there is only a very short pause between flushes. The
semi-double blooms are very large and can reach almost
96mm (4in) across, but they are never crowded on the
truss. They are fragrant and rain resistance is good, so
that all together this is a most welcome addition to the
colour range of bedding roses, particularly for those who
favour soft tones.

Growth is vigorous, with plenty of new canes always
forming and reaching about 75cm (2ft 6in), branching
well and making for a bushy plant. The plentiful, glossy,
light green leaves seem pretty well proof against the
common ills of roses. RNRS Certificate of Merit, 1967.

129

'Evelyn Fison'   Scarlet-red
McGredy, 1962. 'Moulin Rouge' × 'Korona'.

Of all the multitude of dazzling red Floribundas which
have been put on the market over the years, there are
few that can beat this rose. The colour is quite unfading,
even in the strongest sun, and rain does not affect it
either. There can be small, medium-sized and sometimes
very large trusses, which repeat quickly, carrying flowers
on which the petals are attractively waved, though they
have little scent.

Very strong canes on a bushy plant branch out well
and make plenty of new growth each season, reaching
on average about 75cm (2ft 6in). The leaves are on the
small side, and there could sometimes be more of them.
They are very glossy, and though this is often quoted as
one of the healthiest of roses, I have not found it proof
against black spot. The bright colour needs careful
placing in the garden. RNRS Gold Medal, 1963.

'Eye Paint'   Scarlet with white eye and paler reverse McGredy, 1976. ('Little Darling' × 'Goldilocks') × ['Evelyn Fison' × ('Coryana' × 'Tantau's Triumph')].

Almost certainly someone who had not seen this before would be forgiven for wondering if it really was a rose. It makes a very bushy and well-branched plant with masses of mid-green, semi-glossy leaves almost to ground level. Against this background are borne flowers in the greatest profusion in large trusses, single (seven petals) and quite small but of a bright scarlet with a white eye, so that they appear almost to be looking at you. The reverse of the petals is paler and there are pronounced orange stamens. Weather resistance and continuity are both good, but scent is lacking.

As it is such a shrubby grower and will reach 120cm (4ft) quite easily, it is a very good rose for a flowering hedge, but for a general shrub planting some care would be needed, as there are many things that it would not blend too well with. Health on the whole is good. RNRS Trial Ground Certificate, 1973.

'Fragrant Delight'   Coppery orange-salmon
Wisbech Plant Co., 1976. 'Chanelle' × 'Whisky Mac'.

This rose won the RNRS Henry Edland Memorial
Medal for the most fragrant rose under trial in 1976, so
its name is more than apt, and it was also awarded a Trial
Ground Certificate for being a good all-round garden
rose. The blooms are shapely in the bud, and then open
out so that one can see how the coppery orange-salmon
shades to yellow at the centre, around the petal bases.
Small and medium trusses are carried and new ones
form with considerable freedom, giving a long period of
colour – and a colour, too, which is not very common
among the Floribundas. Very strong and well branched
growth will take it up to about 75cm (2ft 6in) or a little
more. Copper tints on the young leaves turn as they
mature to a medium, very glossy green. In general they
are healthy, though mildew late on is not impossible.
Plant 'Fragrant Delight' in a bed under a window that
will be open in the summer so that the scent wafts in.

'Harry Edland' Deep lilac-mauve
Harkness, 1976. ('Lilac Charm' × 'Sterling Silver') ×
['Blue Moon' × ('Sterling Silver' × 'Africa Star')].

Lilac-mauve roses are not usually among the most
popular, largely because most of them in the past have
tended to lose their purity of colour quite quickly and
become a rather dreary grey. They can, too, be
overwhelmed by brighter colours near them, though
mixed with pale yellows, pinks and cream roses they can
look enchanting. However, the deep lilac of 'Harry
Edland' can be relied on to hold well, and the fully
double fragrant blooms come freely in large and small
trusses, which repeat well. Only prolonged rain will
spoil them. This is a tall one as it will go up to 90cm
(3ft), but at the same time it is a well-branched and
bushy grower, excellent for group planting or worth
considering for a hedge. The health of the semi-glossy
leaves is good on the whole, though mildew can be a
possibility. RNRS Trial Ground Certificate, 1975 and
Harry Edland Medal for fragrance.

133

'Iceberg'   White
Kordes, 1958. 'Robin Hood' × 'Virgo'.

The flowers, moderately full, open from pink-tinted
buds, and they are carried in trusses which range from
small to very large, with the blooms always well spaced
out. The scent is not strong, but only continuous rain
will affect the flowers, causing some pink spotting.
Continuity is first-rate, and a great asset is that the
flowers are carried all over the bush at all levels and not
just at the top as in many Floribundas. This makes
'Iceberg' an ideal rose for specimen planting or for
hedges. If lightly pruned it will build up a strong
framework of well-branched canes and will reach up to
150cm (5ft). Harder pruning will keep it down to a
height more suitable for bedding, but it is always a tall
grower. There are very few thorns.

The mid-green, rather pointed, glossy leaves are not
completely proof against either mildew or black spot. It
makes a good standard. RNRS Gold Medal, 1958.

'Irish Mist'   Orange-salmon
McGredy, 1967. Floribunda-Hybrid Tea. 'Orangeade'
× 'Mischief'.

The frilled edges of the petals are a characteristic of this
rose and the blooms are large and Hybrid Tea-like in the
early stages, though they open flat later as they are only
moderately full. They are carried in both large and small
trusses with the flowers nicely spaced. They came freely
and new trusses form with a very satisfying regularity so
that a bed of this variety is seldom without colour. It is
primarily a bedding rose, for it makes a nicely bushy
plant unlikely to go over 75cm (2ft 6in), but very
vigorous within those limits. Rain is no particular
problem to the flowers, but there is only a very slight
fragrance.

Leaf coverage of the bush is good, even though they
are rather on the small side, semi-glossy and an attractive
dark green. The likelihood of mildew is no more than
average, but this is a rose which must be watched for
possible black spot. RNRS Certificate of Merit, 1967.

'Kerryman' Pink with deeper petal edges
McGredy, 1970. Floribunda-Hybrid Tea. 'Paddy Mc-
Gredy' × ('Mme Léon Cuny' × 'Columbine').

This rose can be spaced out a little more widely than
usual if it is used for bedding, as it is a spreading grower,
though by no means a lax one. It forms a wide but still
compact bush which will end up somewhere between
60cm (2ft) and 75cm (2ft 6in) tall, with large, beautifully
shaped flowers in substantial trusses. They are fully
double, and considering their size repeat well. The
deeper pink of the petal edges grows more pronounced
as the flowers age, and the outside of the petals turns
almost red, though the creamy pink of the rest of the
bloom remains. Prolonged rain can spoil the flowers, but
the cooler weather usual in the autumn seems to suit
them particularly well. At all times this is a variety
which makes a particularly lovely vase if picked for the
house, the more so as there are always a lot of flowers
fully out on a truss at one time. Black spot is possible.
RNRS Certificate of Merit, 1971.

'Korresia'   Daffodil yellow
Kordes, 1974. Parentage unknown.

For a reason that cannot be explained satisfactorily by anybody, this rose received no award when it was under trial in the United Kingdom, for it is rapidly being recognized as one of the best bright yellow bedding Floribundas there is and the colour is quite unfading. The flowers are full, having about 35 petals, of high-centred Hybrid Tea form in the early stages and then opening out more with attractively waved petals. Some come singly and some in trusses of five or six, with the possibility of larger trusses later in the season. It is bushy and moderately vigorous, reaching 75cm (2ft 6in) on average, with good, semi-glossy foliage on which disease is rarely seen.

'Korresia' will be almost continuously in flower, and though there can be some damage after prolonged rain, the petals shed cleanly when the blooms are over. Opinions seem to differ about the strength of the fragrance, but the majority view is that it is not strong.

'Lilli Marlene'   Dusky scarlet-red
Kordes, 1959. ('Our Princess' × 'Rudolph Timm') ×
'Ama'.

Dusky crimson shading adds to the attraction of the
glowing scarlet of the moderately full blooms, which
have a soft sheen on the petals when fully open. Fragrance
is only very slight, but rain will do no damage at all.
New trusses form exceptionally quickly so that there is
almost no pause between flushes. Growth is vigorous
and very well branched, though it is on the slender side.
This could be a disadvantage if the trusses were bigger
and heavier, for they might then be weighed down, but
as it is they are as often as not made up of no more than
eight to nine flowers, well spaced out. There are fewer
thorns than average on the red-tinted canes, which take
the rose to about 75cm (2ft 6in). Watch for mildew.

The semi-glossy medium to dark green leaves, red-
tinted when young to match the canes, are bronze-tinted
later. RNRS Certificate of Merit, 1959.

'Living Fire'   Orange, shaded scarlet
Gregory, 1973. 'Super Star' × unknown.

A real eye-catcher and very suitably named, a bed of this
will truly be a 'blaze' of colour, so that if you have a
small garden which you want to be restful, it should be
used with discretion. On the other hand, for a mass
display in a big area there is nothing to beat it, for it will
always be in bloom and is singularly trouble-free. Any
form of disease is a real rarity.

The flowers come both singly and in medium-sized
trusses, quickly repeating. The blooms themselves are
quite large, fully double, and rather on the globular side.
They open quite slowly, and never enough to show the
stamens, retaining what would be called a pompon shape
if they had rather more petals. Rain resistance is good, as
is the autumn flowering, but there is little, if any, scent.
Upright and well-branched growth will reach about
75cm (2ft 6in), with glossy, dark green leaves. RNRS
Certificate of Merit, 1973.

'Margaret Merril' White with pink sheen
Harkness, 1977. Floribunda-Hybrid Tea. ('Rudolph
Timm' × 'Dedication') × 'Pascali'.

'Iceberg' has reigned supreme among white Floribundas
for so long that others, good in their way, such as 'Ice
White', have stood no chance against it and few nurseries
have stocked them. This is a pity for, fine as it is, 'Iceberg'
does have some limitations and there is certainly room
for something as an alternative. The beautiful new
'Margaret Merril' may well be it.

The quite large and very shapely flowers, which are
carried on substantial trusses, are not pure white, though
from a distance they give the impression of being so.
Close up, it can be seen that they have a sheen of satin-
pink, and they are sweetly fragrant. Continuity of bloom
is good, and if there is a weakness it is a dislike of heavy
rain. This is a strong grower, branching out well to
make a bushy plant about 90cm (3ft) tall. A good rose
for a big bed, with dark, glossy leaves. Healthy on the
whole, but mildew possible. RNRS Certificate of Merit,
1978.

'Matangi'
Orange-vermilion with silver eye and reverse
McGredy, 1974. {('Little Darling' × 'Goldilocks') ×
['Evelyn Fison' × ('Coryana' × 'Tantau's Triumph')]}
× 'Picasso'.

There is some variation in the colouring of this rose
according to the time of year, in common with all the
McGredy strain of 'hand-painted' roses which started
with 'Picasso', and the orange-vermilion of the petals
'feathers' rather than merges into the silver central eye,
a most striking effect. In all ways an outstanding rose,
with finely shaped buds opening wide on well-spaced
trusses, unaffected by rain, slightly scented, and coming
with the greatest profusion and continuity. Vigorous
and upright, it will reach 90cm (3ft), branching well to
make a sizeable bush all round. The leaves are coppery
when young, and then turn to a dark, glossy green. Some
black spot has been recorded in the west of England, but
in most places this is one of the healthiest of roses. Its only
real failing is as a cut flower, as it does not take up water
well and the stems droop. RNRS Gold Medal, 1974.

'Memento'   Deep scarlet
Dickson, 1978. 'Bangor' × 'Korbell'.

A new rose of great promise, which has already won high awards in several countries, though not the top one in the United Kingdom. Very free with its flowers in each flush, they also come very quickly again, so much so as to be almost continuous. Of medium size, they open flat and are carried on good trusses. Little scent, but they are unharmed whatever the weather, which does, of course make it a strong recommendation as a bedding rose. Nothing looks worse than a bed of sodden blooms.

The glossy, medium green leaves cover the plant well and its disease resistance is probably a little above average. 75cm (2ft 6in) is the height to be expected, with good strong canes, new ones forming freely and branching out well to form a bushy plant. A variety of considerable merit which was awarded a RNRS Trial Ground Certificate in 1977.

'News' Beetroot purple
Le Grice, 1968. 'Lilac Charm' × 'Tuscany Superb'.

No photograph has so far done justice to 'News'. Neither, really, does the official description which defines it as beetroot purple, for it is much more beautiful than that would imply and unique among roses. One parent is a most unusual one for a Floribunda, the Gallica 'Tuscany Superb', which is a deep maroon-red, but with 'News' something extra has come from somewhere.

The flowers are big and have exceptionally large petals, opening wide to show golden stamens, and are carried on medium-sized trusses. They look particularly well in combination with cream-coloured varieties. Vigorous and compact, it will reach 75cm (2ft 6in) and make a good, bushy plant with plenty of flowers over long periods. The medium green leaves must be watched for black spot. RNRS Gold Medal, 1970.

'Orangeade'   Vermilion
McGredy, 1959. 'Orange Sweetheart' × 'Independence'.

The flowers of this rose, despite its name, could not by
any stretch of the imagination be called orange. They are
rather, when first they open, a glowing deep vermilion
without shadings of any sort and of singular purity,
which does, however, dull a little after a day or so. Fully
70mm (3in) across and semi-double, they are carried on
medium-sized and well-spaced trusses in tremendous
profusion and over a long period in each flush. Hips
form rather readily, so particular attention should be
given to dead-heading to ensure full continuity. There
will be no flower damage through rain, but the blooms
are only slightly fragrant.

Growth is strong, bushy and well-branched, with new
canes forming all though the growing season. 75cm (2ft
6in) is about the average height, and the plentiful, semi-
glossy, mid-green leaves may need protection from black
spot. Not by any means a new variety, it still keeps its
popularity as a sound, reliable bedding rose where
something bright and cheerful but not garish is desired.
RNRS Gold Medal, 1959.

'Paddy McGredy'   Carmine-pink
McGredy, 1962. Floribunda-Hybrid Tea. 'Spartan' ×
'Tzigane'.

An early comer to the now steadily lengthening list of
low-growing roses suitable for small beds in small
gardens, or for front-of-the-border planting. The flowers
are as large as many Hybrid Teas and just as shapely.
They come in medium and fairly large trusses, which
can sometimes be weighed down by the sheer mass of
bloom. Only the slightest of fragrance can be detected
and rain resistance is below average, though it takes
prolonged rain to do real damage. The greatest weakness
is that there will certainly be a long wait between each
flush, which the size of the flowers may have something
to do with.

A 60cm (2ft) but very bushy grower with plentiful
side shoots, it bears dark green, semi-glossy leaves, a little
on the small side. Some mildew and black spot cannot be
ruled out, and this is not a rose for districts where rust is
likely. RNRS Gold Medal, 1961.

'Pink Parfait'   Pink and peach blends
Swim, 1962. Floribunda-Hybrid Tea. 'First Love' ×
'Pinocchio'.

Up until the half-open stage, the flowers resemble
miniature Hybrid Teas, with typical, high, pointed
centres, but later they open out in more conventional
Floribunda fashion. They are carried on trusses which
vary from medium-sized to very large, with the flowers
always well spaced out. The blends of light pink, shading
to creamy-yellow at the petal bases are enchanting at all
stages, and it is very rare for a bloom to be spoiled by bad
weather. A slight fragrance is claimed, but is not easy to
detect. Health is good.

As growth is tall and very freely branching, this will
make a big shrub of 90–120cm (3–4ft), though the canes
are on the slender side so that they may bend under the
weight of the bigger flower trusses. An advantage is that
they are practically thornless. For the back of the border
or for a hedge. RNRS Gold Medal, 1962.

'Priscilla Burton'   Deep carmine with silvery centre
McGredy, 1978. {'Maxi' × ['Evelyn Fison' × ('Orange
Sweetheart' × 'Frühlingsmorgen')]} × {('Little   Dar-
ling' × 'Goldilocks') × ['Evelyn Fison' × ('Coryana'
× 'Tantau's Triumph')] × ('John Church' × 'Elizabeth
of Glamis')}.

'Priscilla Burton' would really have to be quite a rose to
live up to a pedigree like the one shown above, and
fortunately it is just that, the outstanding variety in the
1976 trials, though it was not put on the market until
1978. The flowers are large, on well-spaced trusses, and
open wide to show their silvery centre and prominent
stamens. They are almost petunia-like in their effect if
one can imagine such a thing as a tall petunia bush, for
this is a vigorous, branching grower which will reach
75cm (2ft 6in) or a little more and makes a wonderful
bedding rose. The dark green glossy foliage goes well
with the deep carmine of the petals and is generally
proof against disease. New trusses form freely, so
continuity is very good. RNRS Gold Medal, 1976.

'Queen Elizabeth'   China pink
Lammerts, 1955. Floribunda-Hybrid Tea. 'Charlotte
Armstrong' × 'Floradora'.

For its class, the flowers are very large, and a number
come one to a stem, though the majority are in trusses of
widely varying size. Rain resistance is above average, but
there is little scent. They are, however, very long-lasting
and make ideal flowers to cut for the house. The bushes
can be difficult to place because they are so tall and
upright, forming, if lightly pruned, narrow columns up
to 240cm (8ft) tall with the flowers mainly at the top.
Pruning the canes to different lengths, leaving the
shortest at about 90cm (3ft), will make it bush out rather
more, and in this form it makes a good hedge. The long
stems have very few thorns and bear large, dark green,
glossy leaves, which are extremely healthy. There can be
some blind shoots early on, but if cut back they will
flower. RNRS Gold Medal, 1955. 'Yellow Queen
Elizabeth', a sport, is similar in habit, but not quite so
vigorous.

'Redgold' Golden yellow, edged cherry red
Dickson, 1967. Floribunda-Hybrid Tea. [('Karl
Herbst' × 'Masquerade') × 'Faust'] × 'Piccadilly'.

One of the gayest and most exciting of colour
combinations when first open, the blooms do fade after
a while to an overall pale orange, which is attractive but
less eye-catching. Trusses can at times be very big, but
usually they are of medium size, with the flowers well
spaced out. There is no scent, but also no trouble from
rain.

Strong and upright, this is one of the taller varieties,
probably reaching 90cm (3ft) or a little more, making
it a good hedge rose. It blooms freely and there is plenty
of new growth, quickly produced. The rather small,
mid-green, glossy leaves are red-tinted when young. No
rose in this colour range has yet been produced which is
proof against black spot, and 'Redgold' is no exception.
It is, however, considerably healthier than many others.
Exhibitors find it a good variety in the Floribunda
classes. RNRS Certificate of Merit, 1966.

'Rob Roy'   Scarlet-crimson
Cocker, 1971. Floribunda-Hybrid Tea. 'Evelyn Fison' ×
'Wendy Cussons'.

A rose which is not as well known as it should be, for it
has excellent qualities which make it one of the best for
hedges or for use as a specimen shrub. From this it should
be clear that it is a tall, strong grower with plenty of side
shoots, the ultimate height likely to be at least 90cm
(3ft). A little wider than average planting is advisable,
say about 75cm (2ft 6in).

The flowers are quite full and well-shaped, and the
colour holds well and shows no sign of 'blueing' with
age. Early on, blooms may come two to three to a stem,
but there will be a profusion of medium-sized trusses
later. Flowering is particularly outstanding in cool
weather and rain resistance good, understandable in a
rose of Scottish origin! The semi-glossy, dark green
leaves have crimson tints when they first unfold, and
there is not usually much sign of disease. RNRS Trial
Ground Certificate, 1969.

'Rosemary Rose'   Bright currant red
De Ruiter, 1955. 'Gruss an Teplitz' × a Floribunda
seedling.

It could be argued that this rose should not be a top
recommendation as mildew is almost certain in most
(but not all) situations. However, it is otherwise so
attractive, and is in so many ways unique, that its merits
far outweigh its one and only disadvantage.

There is no other Floribunda of the same bright
currant red, and the 70mm (3in), very full, short-petalled
flowers are in the style of many of the old roses, with
which they consort well. They are carried in huge heads,
in which there will be more than the usual number of
small and medium trusses at one time and at varying
levels, but the growth is fortunately vigorous enough to
support them. The ultimate height is likely to be between
75cm (2ft 6in) and 90cm (3ft).

The leaves are unlike those of any other rose. Many
varieties have red tints when they first unfold, but those
of 'Rosemary Rose' remain a dusky purplish-red for a
considerable period afterwards, only gradually turning
to a very dark matt green. RNRS Gold Medal, 1954.

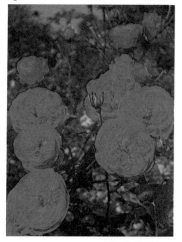

'Sea Pearl'

Pale orange and pink blends with a yellow reverse Dickson, 1964. Floribunda-Hybrid Tea. 'Perfecta' × 'Montezuma'.

The flowers of this variety are as large as some Hybrid Teas. High-centred at first, they soon open cupped, and are carried in trusses of four or five, well spaced out. The colour combination is a particularly attractive one, but there can be some marking of the petals after heavy rain. The scent is only just discernible, and there may be a short pause between each flush of bloom, though it will go on flowering well into the autumn. Growth is tall, upright and vigorous to 90cm (3ft), with strong canes but not a great deal of branching, so that fairly close planting is advised. The leaves are large, plentiful, medium green and glossy, and rarely troubled by disease.

This is probably not a rose to choose for bedding in the mass. It will make a good dividing hedge between one part of a garden and another, but the subtlety of its colourings can, perhaps, best be appreciated if it is planted in groupings of three or four plants and used as a focal point. RNRS Certificate of Merit, 1964.

'Southampton'   Apricot-orange, flushed scarlet
Harkness, 1971. ('Ann Elizabeth' × 'Allgold') × 'Yellow Cushion'.

The large blooms are fairly full, having 26 petals, and are often carried one to a stem early in the year and in medium-sized, well-spaced trusses later on. The petals are slightly frilled and colour stability is good. So is rain resistance and continuity, though the scent is only just detectable. The autumn performance, as so often with roses in the yellow-orange range, is first rate.

This is a very strong grower which, though it will reach 90cm (3ft), is never leggy as there is plenty of side growth. The semi-glossy, dark green leaves are on the small side (perhaps a legacy from 'Allgold) but are abundant, covering the plant well. 'Allgold' may again have passed on another more desirable quality, for 'Southampton' is making a name for itself as one of the healthiest of roses. A singularly trouble-free variety. It makes a good hedge. RNRS Trial Ground Certificate, 1971, but deserved better.

'Stargazer' Orange-scarlet with golden eye
Harkness, 1977. 'Marlena' × 'Kim'.

If you are looking for something small and bright and
cheerful, a rose for a patio garden, for a rockery even, or
for bordering a path where colour but not height is
wanted, this is for you. For 'Stargazer' is compact and
bushy but only reaches about 45cm (1ft 6in) in height.
However, do not be deceived by this into planting it too
closely. 45cm (1ft 6in) is about the distance, as it has
quite a spread despite its dwarf stature. This is not because
of lax canes, for these are always strong and sturdy. The
single flowers with golden zones in the centre are on
trusses in scale with the rest of the plant – in other words
not too large – but there are plenty of them and
continuity is all one could desire. A slight fragrance
only, but first-rate weather resistance.

The leaves are matt and medium green. Generally
they are healthy, but black spot can occur late on. RNRS
Trial Ground Certificate, 1975.

'Stephen Langdon'   Deep scarlet
Sanday, 1969. Floribunda-Hybrid Tea. 'Karl Herbst' ×
'Sarabande'.

This is a rose which created a lot of interest when it first
appeared, as it was and is an absolutely first-rate variety
and one of the healthiest one can grow. For some reason,
however, it never caught the imagination of the public,
which is a great pity. Try it and see how wrong the
public can be.

The flowers open in high-centred, Hybrid Tea form
and have very large petals, which are shown to their full
advantage when they spread more fully later. The rich,
deep colouring is quite unfading to the end, but it should
be said that this rose is one of the later starters in the
summer. The trusses are never large, but seem so because
of the size of the flowers, Some blooms come singly.
Growth is very vigorous and bushy, and very suitable
for bedding. Dark green leaves. RNRS Certificate of
Merit, 1971.

'Sunsilk'   Soft lemon yellow
Fryer, 1974. Parentage unknown.

'Sunsilk' illustrates very well the difficulty in distinguishing between many modern Floribundas and Hybrid Teas. In fact it was originally classified as the latter, but is now generally listed as a Floribunda, by its own raiser among others. It does produce some flowers one to a stem (but then so do many Floribundas, especially early in the season) but the majority come in clusters of four or five. The flowers are full and nicely shaped in the bud, opening more loosely. There is some fade of the soft lemon yellow in hot sunshine, but not enough to spoil the overall effect. There is a slight fragrance.

A vigorous, upright, bushy grower, there will always be plenty of new canes, reaching an average height of about 75cm (2ft 6in), making this a good bedding rose, showy especially in the autumn, when there is little if any colour fade. RNRS Trial Ground Certificate, 1972.

'Topsi' Glowing orange-scarlet
Tantau, 1972. 'Fragrant Cloud' × 'Fire Signal'.

The colour of this rose really glows and seems to be quite unfading, but it is of such a dazzling brightness that care must be taken in placing in relation to other plants. Each of the semi-double blooms is carried on medium-sized trusses on short canes, for this is one of the low-growing, mound-forming roses that suits a small garden or small bed or patio. It is unlikely to go over 45cm (1ft 6in), and is very compact and bushy. Scent is lacking but rain resistance is good. Plenty of new trusses form quickly to keep the flowers coming.

For the size of the plant, the leaves are large, and they are plentiful and well distributed, semi-glossy and mid-green, showing off the blooms well. 'Topsi' gained a RNRS Gold Medal in 1972, but since that time has shown a marked tendency to black spot in certain areas, where die-back can also be a problem on occasion.

157

'Yesterday' Mauveish pink, shading to silvery centre Harkness, 1974. ('Phyllis Bide' × 'Shepherd's Delight') × 'Ballerina'.

Though a Floribunda, 'Yesterday' much more closely resembles one of the smaller China roses in its habit of growth, for it makes a dainty, spreading, wiry shrub reaching possibly 90cm (3ft) and with the racemes of tiny flowers showing all over it at every level in the greatest profusion. It is rare during the summer for no colour to be showing. The leaves are small to match the flowers, are medium green and glossy, taking on a deeper tone in autumn. There will be little trouble from disease.

The colour of the flowers is variable, mauveish pink on opening with silvery petal bases, the main colour changing to lilac pink as the blooms open. They are sweetly scented. This is a rose which will mix well with other border plants, or for planting in groups of three or four, perhaps at the corner of a terrace, rather than for traditional bedding schemes. RNRS Certificate of Merit, 1972.

MINIATURE ROSES (No classification change)

'Baby Darling':   Moore, 1964. 'Little Darling' × 'Magic Wand'. The small flowers vary from orange to orange-pink. Glossy, healthy, dark green leaves. A bushy plant reaching 30cm (12in).

'Baby Masquerade':   Tantau, 1956. 'Tom Thumb' × 'Masquerade'. Similar in effect to the Floribunda 'Masquerade' but colours less harsh, fading from yellow to pink. A tall grower to about 40cm (15in) and freely branched. Some mildew possible.

'Coralin':   Dot, 1955. 'Méphiste' × 'Perla de Alcanada'. Light green, bronze-tinted leaves, on a plant which will reach 30–40cm (12–15in). Large coral-red to orange-red blooms.

'Darling Flame':   Meilland, 1971. ('Rimrose' × 'Josephine Wheatcroft') × 'Zambra'. Profuse double vermilion flowers. Bushy to 35cm (14in).

'Dresden Doll':   Moore, 1975. 'Fairy Moss' × unnamed Moss rose. A breakthrough, in that it is a miniature Moss rose, though it is large for the type, reaching 60cm (2ft). Clusters of quite large, double, soft pink blooms with heavy mossing.

'Eleanor'
(p. 160)

'Fire Princess'

'Easter Morning': Moore, 1960. 'Golden Glow' × 'Zee'. A strong, spreading grower to 30cm (12in) with glossy leaves. The large double flowers are ivory white.

'Eleanor': Moore, 1960. Illustrated on p. 159 (*R. wichuraiana* × 'Floradora') × (seedling × 'Zee'). The full, coral pink blooms are slightly scented. An upright grower to 30cm (12in) with glossy, mid-green leaves. Healthy.

'Fire Princess': Moore, 1969. Illustrated above. 'Baccara' × 'Eleanor'. Very free and continuously in bloom. Orange-scarlet. Bushy to 23cm (9in).

'Golden Angel': Moore, 1975. 'Golden Glow' × unnamed seedling. The flowers have 60–70 petals and are of Hybrid Tea form, some even coming singly. They are bright yellow. Spreading growth to 35cm (14in).

'Gypsy Jewel': Moore, 1975. 'Little Darling' × 'Little Buckaroo'. The blooms are large for a miniature, deep pink and very double, though they are rather loosely formed. They are scented. A strong grower to 30cm (12in).

'Judy Fischer': Moore, 1968. 'Little Darling' × 'Magic Wand'. Healthy, dark, bronze-tinted leaves on a bushy 20–25cm (8–10in) plant. Small, double, rose-pink flowers.

'Lavender Lace':   Moore, 1970. Small, light green leaves on a bushy plant which will average 25cm (10in). Large trusses of very double mauve-lavender blooms.

'My Valentine':   Moore, 1975. 'Little Chief' × 'Little Flirt'. A good, bushy plant reaching 35cm (14in), with bronze-tinted leaves. Double flowers with pointed petals in a rich red.

'Perla de Montserrat':   Dot, 1945. 'Cécile Brunner' × *R. roulettii*. A veteran and still one of the best really small miniatures. The semi-double pink blooms are edged a lighter pearly pink. Dwarf at 23cm (9in) and very compact.

'Pour Toi':   Dot, 1946. 'Edouardo Toda' × 'Pompon de Paris'. The smallest of this selection, only 15–20cm (6–8in) high, but very bushy. Semi-double, the white petals being yellow-tinted at the base.

'Rise 'n' Shine':   Moore, 1977. Illustrated below. 'Little Darling' × 'Yellow Magic'. One of the best of the many yellow miniatures, with an exceptionally clear colour and nicely shaped blooms. Bushy to 35cm (14in).

'Royal Salute':   McGredy, 1976. 'New Penny' × 'Marlena'. Double, carmine-pink blooms in trusses, freely borne. Vigorous, dwarf and compact, with copper-tinted leaves. About 25cm (10in).

'Rise 'n' Shine'

Miniature roses grown in terraced beds at the Royal National Rose Society's gardens in St Albans.

'Stacey Sue': Moore, 1976. 'Ellen Poulsen' × 'Fairy Princess'. Wide-spreading but only reaching about 17–20cm (7–8in) in height. Very double flowers of 60 petals in soft pink come in small sprays.

'Starina': Meilland, 1965. ('Danny Robin' × 'Fire King') × 'Perla de Montserrat'. One of the best and most long-lasting when cut. Vigorous to 25cm (10in), with shapely, bright orange-scarlet flowers.

'Toy Clown': Moore, 1966. 'Little Darling' × 'Magic Wand'. Something different, the semi-double, cupped flowers are white, edged carmine red. 25cm (10in) high.

HYBRID MUSKS (Shrub Roses – Recurrent)

'Ballerina'   Pink, paling towards the centre
Bentall, 1937. Parentage unknown.

The two Hybrid Musks described in this short section
represent the large and the small, for they are a group of
considerable range, almost all of them first-class roses for
hedges, for specimen planting, or in the case of those
comparatively low growing ones, like 'Ballerina', for
bedding. 'Ballerina's' flowers resemble nothing so much
as apple-blossom and are carried in enormous trusses
with great freedom, being both scented and recurrent.
The bush is vigorous and freely-branching, and has
abundant, light green, glossy leaves, which are on the
small side but are generally very healthy. Rain resistance
is particularly good. It is unlikely to exceed 90–120cm
(3–4ft), spreading out to about 90cm (3ft). From this
rose Jack Harkness bred 'Marjorie Fair', which is similar
but the flowers are carmine with a white eye. It received
a RNRS Trial Ground Certificate in 1977.

'Penelope' Blends of creamy white, pink and apricot
Pemberton, 1924. Some doubt about parentage.

One of a large group of Hybrid Musk roses raised at the
beginning of this century by the Rev. Joseph Pemberton,
who gave them their family name, though they are only
very distantly related to the Musk Rose. 'Penelope' forms
a widely branching 210 × 180cm (7ft × 6ft) shrub,
well covered with slightly blue-green, bronze-tinted,
semi-glossy leaves, which are usually very healthy. The
fragrant flowers open loosely, and when they are at the
peak of the summer flush it is difficult to see the bush
beneath them, so profuse are they. They will come again
later, though not in the same overall quantity. However,
it is then more than likely that several long and
enormously vigorous shoots will be sent out, often at
surprising angles, each one bearing trusses of one hundred
or more flowers. Ideal for an informal hedge or for
specimen planting. RNRS Gold Medal, 1925.

MODERN SHRUB ROSES
(Shrub Roses – Recurrent and Non-recurrent)

'Angelina'   Deep pink with light eye
Cocker, 1975. ('Super Star' × 'Carina') × ('Cläre Grammerstorf' × 'Frühlingsmorgen').

This lovely rose is, so far, very little known, though time may change this as it is, in rose terms, a comparative newcomer. If it does catch on it would not by any means be the first variety where a number of years have passed before word-of-mouth recommendation rather than a raiser's promotion has gradually established a rose. It is, in fact, an ideal shrub rose for a small garden, as it forms a vigorous, rounded bush, only 90–120cm (3–4ft) high, spreading out to about 90cm (3ft) in diameter. The whole will be covered with healthy, matt, light green leaves, against which the trusses of 50mm (2in), semi-double, shallowly-cupped flowers show up particularly well. The influence of that fine shrub rose, 'Frühlingsmorgen' shows clearly in them.

'Angelina' makes a good rose for a low hedge, or for planting in the front of the shrub border. It also makes an attractive bed on its own, and is economical to use in this way because of its spread. RNRS Certificate of Merit, 1976.

'Cerise Bouquet'   Cerise-red
Kordes, 1958. *R. multibracteata* × 'Crimson Glory'.

Few people have produced more good, hardy, healthy, modern shrub roses than the German breeder, the late Wilhelm Kordes. Many of them, and 'Cerise Bouquet' is one, are equally at home as short climbers on a pillar or low wall, but when grown as a shrub this one is very large and rambling. Growth is quite open, with long, graceful, arching, thorny canes bearing the stamp of the species parent and reaching 180cm × 180cm (6ft × 6ft). Plentiful grey-green bracts, and the smallish, grey-green leaves derive from the same source. Unlike most of the Kordes hybrids, this one is summer-flowering only, opening its shapely, clustered buds early in the season and carrying on for many weeks. Yellow stamens can be seen when the petals are fully expanded, and there is a rich fragrance. This last is not surprising, as the famous old Hybrid Tea, 'Crimson Glory' (also, incidentally, from Kordes), was one of its parents, still grown today for its scent though there have for long been signs of deterioration in its constitution.

'Chinatown' — Yellow
Poulsen, 1963. 'Columbine' × 'Cläre Grammerstorf'.

Quite a number of modern shrub roses are actually
enormously vigorous Floribundas, and this is one of
them. The habit of growth, with stiff, upright stems, is
typical, and in this case they branch out well and will
reach 120cm (4ft) or so. The blooms are in some ways
like 'Peace', and though not as large, are still very big for
a Floribunda. They are carried in well-spaced trusses of
six or seven, and though they do repeat, there will be a
gap of a few weeks between the first and second flush.
Unlike 'Peace', they are very fragrant, and they stand up
to heavy rain without showing damage of any sort. It
has been said, with in my experience very little
justification, that 'Chinatown' makes more leaves than
flowers. Certainly the large, light green, semi-glossy
foliage is particularly fine and plentiful and extremely
healthy. RNRS Gold Medal, 1962.

167

'Frühlingsgold' Creamy yellow
Kordes, 1937. 'Joanna Hill' × *R. spinosissima hispida.*

'Frühlingsgold' in bloom in late spring and through into early summer is a wonderful sight. Enormously vigorous, the spiny canes rise up from the crown of the plant to 210–240cm (7–8ft), arching over and outwards, borne down by the weight of bloom so that the spread will be something like 180–210cm (6–7ft). Clearly it is not for a patio, but it makes a magnificent specimen planting. The flowers come in small clusters, only just semi-double, with now and then some petaloids (part-formed petals) in the centre, surrounding the amber stamens. They are scented but non-recurrent. The matt, light green leaves are plentiful and extremely healthy.

Not quite so vigorous at 180cm (6ft) is 'Frühlings-morgen' from the same raiser. It is more bushy and branched, with distinctive, lead-green leaves as a background for the large, single, pink flowers, which merge into yellow at the centre and have maroon stamens. With this one there will usually be some later bloom, though not matching the spring display.

'Golden Wings' Soft yellow, deeper at centre
Shepherd, 1956. 'Soeur Thérèse' × (*R. spinosissima altaica* × 'Ormiston Roy').

For a shrub rose of medium size there are few to beat 'Golden Wings' for quality and all-round performance, and it is nowadays being more and more widely planted. It makes a bush about 150–180cm (5–6ft) tall, which branches widely to about the same across, and it has flowers all over it at all levels. These are 70–100mm (3–4in) across, single and sweetly scented, the yellow deepening a little towards the centre, where there are amber stamens. From the yolk yellow buds, the flowers come in clusters in two and possibly three flushes, the first in early summer, and there are usually some flowers in between. Rain does not harm them, and the plentiful, medium-green, matt leaves are rarely troubled by disease. Hips form quite freely, but they are not decorative and should be removed to ensure good continuity. The rose roots easily from cuttings taken in late summer, the resulting plants being just as vigorous as the parent. A certain Gold Medal if it had ever been sent for trial.

'Lavender Lassie'   Soft pink
Kordes, 1959. Parentage unknown.

This has in its time been classed as a Floribunda, and
there is certainly something of a very large Floribunda
about its habit of growth, for it sends up enormously
long 120–150cm (4–5ft) strong, straight canes, bearing
massive heads of flowers at the top of each, with a certain
number of side trusses as well. However, strong as these
canes are, the weight of the flowers is apt to bear them
down towards the ground unless there is some support
from a stake.

Despite its name, it is rare to find any colour other
than pink in the short-petalled, pompon style blooms,
and this fades a little – though quite pleasantly – in hot
sun. Nor is it easy to detect the strong scent often claimed
for this rose, but the flowers do stand rain exceptionally
well considering how double they are, and they are
profuse and recurrent. The leaves are a bright, light,
glossy green, and are very healthy. RNRS Trial Ground
Certificate, 1959.

'Magenta'   Rosy purple and mauve blends
Kordes, 1955.   Floribunda   seedling × 'Lavender
Pinocchio'.

Another rose which has a name which does not really match the colour, in this case rather fortunately. The flowers are very double and with short centre petals so that they open cupped to flat. The clusters are not usually of more than four or five blooms, but there are plenty of them, and flowering is very continuous, right through to the autumn. The fragrance is outstanding.

In theory, this rose should reach 120–150cm (4–5ft), but the freely-branched canes are so slender and lax, that it will only do so if well staked or grown on a tripod. It must have support of some sort if the flowers at the ends of the canes are to be kept from dragging on the ground. The leaves are matt, dark green and have bronze tints. Some precautions against mildew and black spot are advisable. Sometimes 'Magenta' will be classed among the Hybrid Musks, but its connection with them is tenuous to say the least.

'Nevada'   Creamy white
Dot, 1927. Possibly 'La Giralda' × a *moyesii* seedling.

If they could pick only one shrub rose, old or new, this
would be the choice of many, provided that they had
room for it. It will grow into a great mound of long,
arching but well-branched plum-red canes fully 240cm
(8ft) high and about the same across, and in late spring
and early summer every single shoot will be weighed
down by the mass of 100–120mm (4–5in) single flowers,
so closely spaced that they overlap each other and
completely hide the branches beneath. It is a sight that
once seen, is never forgotten, and there are usually some
flowers, though nothing like as many, later on as well.
All they lack for perfection is scent.

The leaves are small, rather rounded in outline, and a
darkish blue-green. There can be some black spot, but
this is rarely serious. In 1959 a pink sport of 'Nevada'
appeared in Hilling's nursery, and was named 'Marguerite
Hilling'. It is almost equally good.

'Nymphenburg' Pale salmon-pink with yellow tints
Kordes, 1954. 'Sangerhausen' × 'Sunmist'.

Vigorous and upright to 180cm (6ft) and eventually
arching over and branching out to a spread of about
120cm (4ft), this is tremendously free-flowering, with
enormous heads of many blooms, opening first in early
summer and carrying on well into the autumn. After a
hot summer to ripen them, there will be orange-red
hips, so dead-heading should be done after the first flush
to make sure of plenty of later flowers. Health is good on
the whole, though there can be black spot after
midsummer. The leaves are plentiful, large, dark green
and glossy, framing attractively the double, scented
flowers, in which the blends of pink and pale orange
merge into yellow at the petal bases, a very lovely
combination. A wonderful rose for a flowering hedge,
for planting in the mass in a large border, and it will
make a handsome specimen. This is a modern rose which
will blend very happily if planted with the once-
flowering old roses, extending the blooming period of
a mixed collection. RNRS Trial Ground Certificate,
1954.

THE ROSE IN THE GARDEN

BEDDING

Roses should always be grown where they will have plenty of sun and, provided this is done, they make ideal bedding plants. If Floribundas or some of the lower-growing China roses are chosen, they will be more or less continuously in flower for five or six months of the year, which little else can match. Most Hybrid Teas are not quite so prolific with their bloom, and with them there may well be a period of rest in the middle of the summer, but they are well worth while using just the same for their sheer beauty.

In a small bed with perhaps only a single or a double row of roses, mixed varieties and colours can look quite well, provided that they all grow to more or less the same height. Medium-sized or large beds with mixed varieties can, at certain times, look rather 'spotty', as the flowering time of different roses varies. A lot of the time they will all be out, but at other times only some of them. If, however, you do wish to have different colours, it is best to plant in groups of not less than four to five of each variety, giving particular care to the harmonious blending of tones. Roses come, for instance, in a bewildering number of reds, anything from the brightest scarlet to deep crimson, and one of these can easily kill the other. Cream, white or pale yellow roses make good 'dividers' between colours that might otherwise clash. It is best to avoid a mixture of Hybrid Teas and Floribundas in the same bed, as their habits of growth and flower types are so dissimilar.

For a really gay effect, a circular bed can be used, divided into four or five segments with a different,

Beds with a mixture of standard and bush roses.

though blending, colour in each, and perhaps with a standard or pillar rose in the centre to give height. A number of beds, all reaching about the same level, can be monotonous. The eye likes a change, and a row of standards (in the same or contrasting hues) down the centre of a long bed will make a tremendous difference.

For bedding, always choose varieties which are reasonably uniform and bushy growers. Tall, leggy roses are for the back of the border with something else in front. Generally speaking, the smaller the bed, the smaller the roses you should choose for it, and the owners of small and patio gardens are nowadays in luck. In recent years nurseries have been introducing more and more varieties that form cushions of colour no more than 60cm (2ft) high, and in many lists they are actually called patio roses.

How close one should plant roses in a bed must depend to some extent on how the variety one has chosen grows. A widely branching, or a sprawling one, needs more room than one that keeps narrow and upright. 45–60cm (18in to 2ft) can be taken as a good average distance between plants if you are unsure as to how a rose will behave.

HEDGES

Roses make some of the most colourful – and thorny – hedges there are, though they are not, of course, evergreen. They can range from garden dividers about 45cm (18in) high – Polyanthas, through 60–90cm (2–3ft) Floribundas and Hybrid Teas, to various shrub roses such as the Rugosas and Hybrid Musks for 150–180cm (5–6ft) boundary hedges. No other shrub will give the same quantity and continuity of bloom, and with the Rugosas autumn leaf colour and huge scarlet hips are a late bonus. With none of them, however, should one expect the squared-off outline of a privet or beech. Their informality of habit is half their charm, so use secateurs to trim them, not shears. Staggered planting in two rows on centre lines about 30cm (1ft) apart will give a thicker hedge, though this should not be needed with shrub roses which on their own may reach 120–150cm (4–5ft) across.

ROSES FOR HEDGES
Short: about 30cm (1ft)
'The Fairy'   Most miniatures

Medium height: 90–150cm (3–5ft)

'Alexander'   'Iceberg'
'Angelina'   'Officinalis'
'Ballerina'   'Peace'
'Chinatown'   'Pink Parfait'
'Dame of Sark'   'Redgold'
'English Holiday'   'Rob Roy'
'Eye Paint'   'Rosa Mundi'
'Frau Dagmar Hastrup'   'Southampton'
'Harry Edland'

Tall: 150–210cm (5–7ft)

R. × *alba maxima*   'Queen Elizabeth'
R. × *alba semi-plena*   'Roseraie de l'Hay' (and
'Nymphenburg'   most other Rugosas)
'Penelope' (and most other   'Yellow Queen Elizabeth'
    Hybrid Musks)

STANDARDS

How Hybrid Tea and Floribunda standards can be used with bedding roses has been mentioned on p. 175, and there are, in fact, three heights available, those with 105cm (3ft 6in) stems (full), those with 75cm (2ft 6in) stems (half) and quarter standards with 45cm (18in) stems. Using all three it is possible to make a spectacular bed against a wall with the tallest at the back, half standards in front of them, and quarter standards in front yet again. A low lavender hedge would finish it off admirably, or a row of low-growing bush roses.

Standards can also be used for specimen planting on their own, either to fill up a dull corner where two hedges meet, or in a small, circular bed in the middle of a lawn. Choose a variety which makes a big head, but even more spectacular (though once-flowering if the variety used is a rambler) will be the tallest type of standard of all, the weeping standards on 150–180cm (5–6ft) stems.

CLIMBERS AND RAMBLERS

There is nothing like a climbing rose for brightening up a wall, but despite what some nursery catalogues say, no climber is really perpetual in its flowering. Some, of course, do not repeat at all, but with those that do there is generally a spectacular first flush of bloom followed by several weeks with nothing but a few odd flowers, and then in late summer or early autumn a second but less profuse show. So there will be periods with no colour and the answer is, if this does not content you, to grow the roses up through other flowering wall shrubs with different flowering periods. An alternative is to grow something like a clematis up through them.

Chaenomeles (Japonica) or *Forsythia suspensa* will flower before the roses; various kinds of Ceanothus bloom either before, with, or after, and the powdery blue of many of the latter looks remarkably well with white roses like 'Swan Lake' or pale yellow ones like 'Casino'. A number of the large-flowered clematis come into bloom later in the summer when most climbing roses rest, but if they are used they must be properly cut back at the end of winter if they are not to develop into an impenetrable tangle and smother the plants which support them.

There are many short climbing roses nowadays, like 'Golden Showers' or 'Clair Matin', which will not go much over 240cm (8ft), and which are particularly useful if you live in a bungalow with limited wall space. Most of them can also be planted as rather lax, undisciplined shrubs without any support at all, and they are of great value as pillar roses, which have much the same function in a garden as standards, either to give height or to be used for specimen planting. A rose which will reach 6m (20ft) up a wall is not the thing for a 240cm (8ft) pillar, or for a tripod made of rustic poles, which is an alternative to a pillar but gives greater scope for training because there is more of it.

Ramblers are not suitable for walls. They are for pillars, tripods, trellis-work fences, arches and pergolas, combined again with other climbers if you wish. They (and climbers) will also help to hide an unsightly garden shed, but perhaps the most exciting way to grow them is up trees. Their flexible canes are ideal for weaving through the branches, and especially with some of the older Musk ramblers, huge heads of bloom will hang down in a creamy waterfall, scenting the air all around. Choose a very robust tree for these, however, for the weight and wind resistance of some of the more vigorous of these roses is enormous. An old, half-dead apple tree is not the thing to use. Plant a rambler on the windward side of a tree, so that the new canes will blow in towards it rather than away.

SHRUB ROSES

There are two popular misconceptions about shrub roses for the garden which it would be as well to deal with straight away. The first is that they only flower once in a season.

This is true of almost all species, and of the Gallicas, Damasks, Albas, Centifolias and most Moss roses, but not of the China roses, Rugosas, Hybrid Musks and the majority of modern shrub roses. Bourbons in general are recurrent (they were the first of the Western hybrids to be so), and so are most Hybrid Perpetuals, though it is true that the autumn flowering may not match that of midsummer.

From this it can be seen that the split is fairly even between those that flower more than once a year and those that do not, but even with those that do put on a single display, this will be a really spectacular one which will last for many weeks. It would be an exceptional lilac or rhododendron which could beat it.

The second misconception is that all shrub roses are too big for a small garden, but there are many examples from all the groups which will grow no more than

150cm (5ft) tall by about 90cm (3ft) wide. Among the Spinosissimas (which are species roses) and the Gallica and China rose families particularly, a great number are smaller still, and the last two can be used for bedding or the front of a shrubbery.

The larger species make excellent specimen shrubs planted on their own or, provided that they have plenty of sun, they can be mixed in a general shrub planting, flowering early and, in some cases, giving late colour as well with their hips. Many will scramble up through their neighbours with delightful informality, and will greatly enhance the rather sombre foliage of evergreens such as a holly.

A number of the Albas and Damasks also make large bushes, and these can be used in much the same way as species, but whereas the bigger Albas are very robust, tall and upright, the Damask growth is likely to be more lax and spreading. If the Albas are growing on their own roots, they may spread slowly by suckering, so some allowance should be made for this when allocating them space.

Neither the Albas nor the Damasks should need artificial support, but as was mentioned in the description of 'Fantin Latour' (p. 54), the natural habit of the canes and flowers of the Centifolias is to droop. To be able to appreciate their beauty to the full, the stems must be held erect, and if this is done they will blend excellently, peony-like, in a bed of mixed perennials. The tallest of all should be displayed on a pillar or tripod.

Pillars and tripods, set in a bed or in a lawn, are also useful for tying in many of the more rampantly vigorous Bourbons, and if space is limited a degree of training will keep them much more under control. Using them as short climbers on a wall or fence is an alternative, remembering however, that they will bush out considerably and not just go up and up like a true climber, which makes them unsuitable near a narrow path beside a house. Some Hybrid Perpetuals can be treated in the same way as the middle range (by size) of the Bourbons. There are shorter varieties that will grow like the taller Hybrid Teas and can be used for bedding, while those with the very long canes and flowers just at the top should be pegged down (see 'Baronne Prévost', p. 63). Alternatively, they can be tied down to a low wire framework covering the whole of the bed, with a very pleasing effect.

Rugosas and Hybrid Musks are primarily specimen or hedging roses, early and continuously in bloom, with the former group having the best and healthiest foliage there is, together with spectacular hips. With rose hedges, other than those formed from the upright-growing Floribundas, allowance must be made for considerable width. However, provided it is done from the beginning, the fairly rigid canes of the Hybrid Musks can be trained on wires strung between rustic poles, though even then they are likely to send strong shoots out at unexpected angles.

All shrub roses – in fact all roses – look particularly well interplanted and mingled with grey or grey-green leaved plants such as rosemary or lavender, and tall white lilies thrusting up through the wide-ranging, lax canes of one of the Damask roses for instance, give a striking contrast in flower form.

MINIATURE ROSES

Because they are so small and fragile-looking, it is often thought that miniatures are not as hardy as other roses. The fact that they are often sold in pots encourages the view that they are house, or at the very least greenhouse, plants, but both ideas are wrong. Miniatures are much more at home in the open garden than the house, where the atmosphere is likely to be much too dry for them and will probably cause the leaves to fall. They are sold in pots because it is a convenient way of handling and displaying them, but they should only be taken indoors when the flower buds are just opening, and be removed outside again to recover the minute blooming is over.

In the garden, miniature roses have many uses, some of them depending on how tall particular varieties grow, for they do vary. Quite a number, while still keeping their small leaf and flower size, will reach 25–30cm (10–12in), and a few will go up to 40cm (15in). Probably the majority are about 23cm (9in), and there is a select minority which really are miniatures at 15–20cm (6–8in).

The taller miniatures, such as 'Starina' (orange-vermilion) or 'Easter Morning' (cream), are admirable for a small bed or for lining paths or drives. All these little roses begin to flower before the Hybrid Teas and Floribundas, and in a good season will carry on until late in the autumn, giving very good value in the mass. One way of bringing them nearer to eye-level so that the daintiness of their individual blooms can be appreciated and the fragrance of some of them given full value, is to grow them in terraced beds with brick or stone retaining walls, as in the picture on p. 162. Miniature standards can be used to add variety, with climbing miniatures such as 'Nozomi' to ramble down the walls themselves. The climbers could also be grown up trellises at the back, but for them a word of warning is needed. Many are far more vigorous in relation to the bush miniatures than full-sized climbers are to Hybrid Teas or Floribundas, and may easily reach 150–180cm (5–6ft). Allow them plenty of room.

Clumps of miniatures, from the tall to the very tiny ones, make excellent plants for a rockery. Most alpines are early-flowering, so they give a touch of colour later, but they must have deep pockets of good soil to grow in and a cool root run.

An equally effective use for miniature roses is in window-boxes or stone or wooden sinks and troughs on a patio. These must be well drained and not less than 23cm (9in) deep. Put a layer of broken crocks or rubble along the bottoms to keep the drain holes clear and fill with any good potting mixture, or a mixture of soil and peat in equal quantities. Keep them well watered in dry spells, and add a slow-acting rose fertilizer twice a year.

GROUND-COVER

There are a number of roses which can be used for ground-cover, for smothering weeds. A species rose which mounds itself up into a vast 240cm × 240cm (8ft × 8ft) tangled shrub will do this, of course, but a real ground-cover rose will not only spread widely but be low-growing as well. It can be used for covering rough banks in a garden which, because of their slope, are difficult to keep tidy with a lawnmower, or to hide in an attractive way any piece of waste ground which is not in full shade. Two different types of rose are involved, and both are non-recurrent.

R. wichuraiana has already been mentioned on p. 22, and though this will scramble upwards through surrounding shrubs or on artificial supports, its natural habit is to creep gradually along the ground, rooting as it goes where it touches the earth. Given time, it will form a fairly dense mat of shiny green leaves, which the white, single, starlike flowers will light up in the middle of summer. To obtain a reasonably even coverage, it is likely that some of the canes will need pointing in the right direction from time to time.

Apart from this rose, several rambler hybrids, such as 'Max Graf' (pink) and 'Temple Bells' (white) are equally effective, but with them all perennial weeds such as couch-grass must be kept in check in the rose's early years. If once established and rampant, it would take more than one of these roses to eradicate such weeds completely. Rambler hybrids will continue to spread indefinitely until checked by secateurs, but they will rarely exceed 60–90cm (2–3ft) in height.

Details of the second kind of ground-cover rose can be found on p. 46 under *R. × paulii rosea*. With them it is not a case of a rose spreading out to form a multitude of plants, but of one bush which grows not more than 90–120cm (3–4ft) high, but covers perhaps 3.6m (12ft) of ground with its long, interweaving, pendulous canes. Beneath them few weeds can survive.

186

Notes

Notes

Notes

Notes